Voigtländer And I: In Pursuit Of Shadow Catching : A Story Of Fifty-two Years' Companionship With A Camera...

James Fitzallan Ryder

James F. Ryder

URSUIT OF ...

Story of Fifty ... Ye...

with a Cam...

By ...JAMES...

CLEVELAND, O.
The Cleveland Printing & Publishing
The Imperial Press
1902

Voigtländer and I

IN PURSUIT OF SHADOW CATCHING

A Story of Fifty-Two Years' Companionship

with a Camera

By *JAMES F. RYDER*

CLEVELAND, O..

THE CLEVELAND PRINTING & PUBLISHING CO.

The Imperial Press

1902

IN LOVING MEMORY

OF HER WHO USED TO TUCK TWO YOUNG BOYS

IN THEIR TRUNDLE-BED AT NIGHT,

AND WHILE THEY SLEPT,

DARNED THEIR STOCKINGS AND PATCHED

THEIR MUCH WORN BREECHES,

THIS BOOK IS INSCRIBED.

CONTENTS.

P. T. Barnum. A Familiar Character. A Letter from Petroleum V. Nasby. "Papa Cramer." Analogy Between Sound and Color. Sam Briggs. "Little Pitchers Have Big Ears." Uncle Brewster's Photograph. Muskingum Bridge. Good-Bye, "Uncle Ryder."

INTRODUCTION.

DETROIT, July 11, 1902.

MY DEAR MR. RYDER:—

When first Old Sol consented to be a partner with man and lend his aid to capture and hold the fleeting image of prattling childhood, ambitious youth and modest maiden, a father's pride and a mother's charms, or grand, glorious old age, who, looking back with no regrets, looks forward to the golden promises that crown a life well spent, he little dreamed, perhaps, of the everlasting boon conferred upon the world.

Little by little Dame Nature gave, often grudgingly, of her secrets, so that by and by out of the dim shadows there came substance and reality.

No longer need we wander with tear-dimmed eyes through the empty halls of memory, vainly seeking by their echoes some semblance to the faces of those we have loved and lost, for now upon the printed page their counterparts smile and smile again as of yore.

Painted canvas may give us the bloom of youth, may scatter over the head of age winter's hoary frost, but for truth of feature wherein beams anew the very soul of the sitter, we lovingly turn to those masterpieces painted by the subtle fingers of the god of day.

It falls to the lot of but few mortals that their span of life should reach from the beginning to the present of the art of photography, but within the covers of this book the reader may wend his way in most pleasant companionship. Tried and true friends are " *Voigtländer* and I " who, David-and-Jonathan-like, have trod life's rugged highway. Misty morning, noonday sun, and evening splendor found them worshiping at the shrine of earthly beauty, honesty, and truth, giving to their creations that eternal stamp of character that made the subjects live.

And now, sitting on the sixty-fifth milestone, these two old chums, " *Voigtländer* and I," recount in simple, heartfelt words the story of their struggles, their hopes, their failures, and their achievements. May the story prove as delightful, as entertaining, as encouraging and profitable to others as it has to me is the sincere, earnest, honest wish of   Your friend,

A. H. GRIFFITH.

PREFACE.

VOIGTLÄNDER came of a good house, a noted ancestry, and a long line. He first saw light at Vienna, Austria.

We drifted together in '47, since when we have been staunch friends; a truer, more constant or reliable one I never had.

He was truth itself. What he told me was as gospel. No misrepresentations, no deceits, no equivocations. He saw the world without prejudice; he looked upon humanity with an eye single to justice. What he saw was faithfully reported, exact, and without blemish.

He could read and prove character in a man's face at sight. To his eye a rogue was a rogue; the honest man, when found, was recognized and properly estimated. His devotion to me was constant and without limit. My love for him was sincere.

If I was sometimes whimsical or cranky and implied blame to him, there was no retaliation, no word in justification or reproach,— just the bland, quiet submission which distinguished his even balance was maintained. The dear old considerate friend put me to shame.

I may as well say at once, " Voigtländer " was my camera, and I am,

Yours truly,

JAMES F. RYDER.

NOTE.—To Mr. Charles Orr, Librarian of Case Library, Cleveland, O., Mr. James R. Hale, also of Case Library, and Mr. Augustus Wintemberg, of The Imperial Press, Cleveland, O., I make grateful acknowledgment for courtesies received.

VOIGTLÄNDER AND I.

CHAPTER I.

THE EARLY DAGUERREOTYPE.

The first daguerreotype I ever saw was shown me by Mrs. Jack Masten, our nearest neighbor, who came bursting into our house one morning as excited as a child, to show my mother a new wonder she had just received from New York. It was a likeness of her sister, Miss Julia Turnbull, a ballet dancer of the New York theaters. The letter accompanying and explaining this likeness said it was a new discovery by a Frenchman named Daguerre, and the picture was called daguerreotype. The process for producing the newly discovered method was brought from Paris to New York by Prof. S. F. B. Morse, the father of telegraphy. The likeness I saw was taken by a Mr. Plumb, who had just opened a studio on Broadway. That picture was the first image I had ever beheld made by a camera. I had never seen a camera and would not have known what it was had one been placed before me. The picture was a wonder to me, and as the first will always be remembered. I recall with distinctness how it looked, can see how the hair was braided, and that she wore a low-neck dress. Suspended from a chain about her neck was a handsome locket. Altogether she was a bright looking and pretty girl. I thought the picture fine and carried the remembrance of it in my mind as a mental study, striving to make my own work resemble it. In after years, the same Julia Turnbull, whom I had never met in person, came into my gallery in Cleveland to have photographs taken. She had grown away from the bare shoulders period and abandoned the locket. She knew nothing of the part her daguerreotype had played in my early struggles as a learner. She seemed like an image risen out of the past, which had been something to me " once upon a time."

So startling a discovery as the daguerreotype created much interest in all cities where it was introduced. The absolute truthfulness of resemblance to the person taken was remarkable.

Visitors to New York sometimes, brought home with them a likeness of themselves, as a novelty and a wonder to their friends. After a time the "daguerrian artist," so-called, began to manifest himself in the small cities and towns about 'the country, and his coming was quite an event.

THE PROFESSOR.

Along in the forties many daguerreotype men styled themselves "professor," and their titles were seldom questioned. It was but a step from the anvil or the sawmill to the camera. The new business of likeness-taking was admitted to be a genteel calling, enveloped in a haze of mystery and a smattering of science. The dark room where the plates were prepared was dignified by some of the more pretentious as the laboratory. A "No Admittance" door, always carefully closed by "the professor" on entering or emerging, naturally impressed the uninitiated as something out of the usual, and when he came out carrying a little holder to his sitter and from it drawing a thin slide, revealing from under it the likeness just taken, it was no unreasona-

This is a copy of a daguerreotype of the first human face taken with a camera—Dorothy Elizabeth Draper, taken by her brother, Professor John W. Draper, in New York City, in the year 1840. Used by permission and courtesy of *The Photographic Times-Bulletin*, New York City.

ble stretch of credulity to recognize in the man something of a scientist and a professor. In the fall of 1847 I met the professor who was to lead me into the mysteries of daguerreotypy. I had been three years the boy behind the press, pushing the inking roller over the pages of "forms" in a book-printing office, with a vague idea of following the Ben Franklin route, when I met Professor Brightly, a newcomer to our village, a daguerreotype man. He encouraged my visits to his rooms, and I naturally became interested in the new and mysterious work. Professor Brightly was a tall man of rather striking appearance. His silk hat had been much brushed and was shiny. He wore glasses, his hair was heavy, stiff, and, especially in front, stood straight up. At the sides it was trained behind his ears, at the back it covered his coat collar. His eyes were gray and keen, which evidently pleased him. He had a big forehead, bigger up and down than across. He wore a large gray shawl, heavily folded, such as was worn by men fifty years ago as a shoulder covering and as a substitute for an overcoat. His trousers bagged at the knees and were too short by a couple of inches. He always wore rubbers.

He had taught cross-roads school in the country, had a smattering knowledge of and had lectured upon phrenology and biology. The new art of daguerreotypy attracted his attention and had been gathered in as another force with which to do battle in the struggle for fame and dollars. His habit of brushing with his hand the already stiff front hair in an upward direction rather emphasized its standing and his dignity.

Photograph by J. C. Strauss, St. Louis, Mo.

His manner was genial, meant to impress the person in his

presence that, although a professor, he did not choose to se-
clude himself in his superior knowledge to the exclusion of his
surroundings. He was a sun that could afford to shine upon
other and lesser planets without dimming its own luster. In
a friendly way he had felt my bumps, found ideality prominent,
color good, form excellent, and assured me that I was a promising
subject and would make a mark as a daguerreotypist. He knew I
had a little money which he wished to lure from my pockets into
those trousers of his with the baggy knees. He flattered me and I
succumbed; that's how it happened that I took to the camera.
Whether it may have been a disappointment to my father that his
firstborn son had no higher aspirations than making likenesses with
a little box machine I know not. He was a man of few words,
but he helped me to pay for my outfit and wished me success. I
was a proud young man to be possessor of a camera, and *my
Voigtlander* was even better than the professor's, a great prize
indeed for those times, but a very primitive affair as considered
with the outfits of the present day. The camera was perched upon
a tripod of turned maple legs, which screwed into sockets of iron,
with a collar or tubing through which passed, up or down, the
upright post for raising or lowering the instrument, and which
fastened at any point by a thumbscrew. Such was the mechanical
device for holding. On top of the post was a wee platform with
hinges at front and a wooden screw at the back for raising or lowering it to give pitch to the camera itself. I can picture it in my
mind's-eye now as plainly as though I had seen it last week. I
can see its rosewood veneer, the edges at front and back chamfered
to an angle of forty-five degrees; its sliding inside box, with the
focusing glass which was drawn up and out of the top through
open doors and the plateholder was slid down into its place. These
doors were hinged to open one toward the front and the other
toward the back, each having a little knob of turned bone by which
to lift it, and there were two little inset knobs of the same material
turned into the top of the box upon which the knobs of the doors
should strike, and the concussion of those bone knobs more than
fifty years ago is remembered today as plainly as though I had
been hearing them every day from then until now; while the odor
of iodine from the coated plates in that dear old box lingers with
me like a dream. The box was the body, the lens was the soul,
with an "all-seeing eye," and the gift of carrying the image to the
plate. I entertained great reverence for my lens, for we would go

P. S. Ryder, Photographer. Syracuse, N. Y.

THINKING OF SANTA CLAUS.

out into the world together some day; we would see a bit of it, at least, and possibly learn the color of its coin. I was required by the professor to do the general chore work about the place, under the assumption that to start at " the foot of the ladder " was the correct way to commence any profession. While the boy spirit secretly kicked at the drudgery, the discretion of the coming man was exercised to keep silence. I learned later that a young man willing to do anything required of him pertaining to the work at which he was employed found the best chance to progress. To be trusted, to be found worthy, to be depended upon, is a strong pull for any young man entering upon a career. To be useful to his employer is an assurance of advancement.

My teacher now showed me step by step the routine of making a daguerreotype, and I availed myself as best I could of the knowledge he imparted. The plates used were of copper body and silver surface, upon which the image or likeness was received. The surface of the plate was carefully scoured with fine rottenstone sifted through muslin of close texture and wet with alcohol. A pad of Canton flannel with long and close nap was used as a polisher. It was next buffed with buckskin and rouge until the surface was polished as finely as a mirror. It was now ready for the chemical coating that rendered it sensitive to the action of light. The coating boxes contained glass jars carefully ground at the top, and fitted to slabs of glass also ground, which were made to slide over the top of the jars. When closed, the ground surfaces of the jar top and the covering slab fitted as tightly as stoppered bottles. One of these jars had flakes of resublimed iodine sprinkled over the bottom, from which fumes steadily rose. The other contained a mixture of bromine and chlorine, called " quick stuff," which also constantly gave off fumes. When sufficiently polished for the coating, the plate was adjusted to a small carrying-frame or kit, in the sliding cover, and was then passed over the fumes of the iodine to take its first coating. When it assumed a golden yellow color it was exposed to the fumes of the " quick," or accelerator, until it attained a rose color, then back again a moment over the iodine to secure a harmonious blending of bromo-iodine and then it was ready for exposure on the sitter through the lens of the camera. When the sitter was comfortably and gracefully posed, the light and shade properly distributed, the focal adjustment of the lens made to show clearly the features, the exposure was made. Up to this point no image was visible upon the plate, but exposure to the

H. H. Pierce, Photographer, Providence, R. I.

"HERE IT COMES!"

fumes of heated quicksilver in a bath for the purpose developed the image, and a most interesting sight it was to watch the image coming out of a blank plate and gradually revealing the form and features as they came into being.   In the earlier days, when only iodine was used as a sensitizer, a long time was required to impress the plate.   The poor martyr who sat for an hour in direct sunlight was paying dearly for his likeness.   When bromine was discovered to be an accelerator to speed in the process, the time of sitting was reduced from one hour to one minute, a great stride in advancement.

The professor was anxious for my progress and helped me all he could.   He encouraged me, praised my work as promising and satisfactory, assured me I was surprisingly good for a beginner, and told me it would be greatly helpful for me to work out the difficulties alone, rather than depend upon him. The fact was, I asked too many questions, many of which he could not answer. In the first few years most practitioners were plodding in the dark, something like " the blind leading the blind." There was no literature bearing upon the subject beyond the mere statement of routine description, no sure road yet opened to successful work. " Professors " were more plentiful than intelligent teachers. In our work repeated trial was the rule — we would try and try again without knowing the cause of failure. Many a day did I work blindly and almost hopelessly, pitying my outraged sitters, and pitying myself in my despair and helplessness. The weak excuses and explanations I made to cover my ignorance were many. The lies I told, if recorded, would make a big book which I would dislike to see opened. " *You moved!* " headed the list. " You looked too serious!" " You did not keep still!" " You winked too often!" These and other fabrications to show the necessity for another sitting were made with great efforts at cheerfulness, but the communings with my inner self in the dark room while preparing the next plate would hardly bear the light, and were best left in the dark. After three months' practice I had gained confidence and some skill. The professor could and did trust me with his business when on occasion he went out to arrange for and deliver lectures in the neighboring villages. These lecture outings were productive of advantage to the business in daguerreotypes. He made acquaintances who came in for likenesses and in turn the picture business played into the hands of the lecture field. We were not accused of driving " a trust " or " a combine," but photography, phrenology, and biology were all handled from our headquarters at 137 Owego street, over J. M. Heggies' harness store, Ithaca, New York. It was no uncommon thing to find watch repairers, dentists, and other styles of business folk to carry daguerreotypy " on the side." I have known blacksmiths and cobblers to double up with it, so it was possible to have a horse shod, your boots tapped, a tooth pulled or a likeness taken by the same man; verily, a man — a daguerreotype man, in his time, played many parts.

CHAPTER II.

MR. SHAW GOT LONESOME.

I remember one day the Professor was sent for from one of his lecturing stands to go and take a picture of a young child that had died, and he took me along to assist. It was my first experience in such work, and I was glad to go. The child was a dear little girl, and we arranged her upon a couch as though in sleep, with a rosebud in her dimpled hand, an expression of peace in her pure face, as a reflection of Heaven. The parents concluded, since we were there, to have pictures of their other children. A camera had never been seen there before, and a number of other persons desired to be taken. We were obliged to stop over until the next day to do the work, and I was sent back to town for more plates and cases, a trip which took me half the night to perform. We took as many as a dozen persons, among whom was a bluff old fellow named Shaw. We took him and his wife, Mehitable. Mrs. Shaw died suddenly a few weeks afterward. Mr. Shaw came into our studio his next visit to town, seeming much bereaved. He expressed himself as " very thankful that he had gotten the picture; it was a blessed comfort to him." A few months later he came again, this time accompanied by a young, bashful-acting girl, who looked both happy and embarrassed. Mr. Shaw said, " We want our pictures taken, both together, me holding her hand." Continuing, he said, " This is a fresh one. She's my neighbor's daughter. Ain't she pretty?" And he pinched her cheek in a fondling way. As though his mind was recalling the past he said, " Mehitable was a powerful good woman. She's been gone now nigh onto a year, and I got lonesome " — and, in the blush of his honeymoon, he called up a little sigh, then said, " Come on, sis," and together they went romping down the stairs like a pair of happy children.

And now came into our village a rival daguerreotypist, Professor Bartholomew, and he looked dangerous. He was past middle life, a man of polished manners and fashionable dress. He wore a loose overcoat with fur collar and cuffs, great frogs of braid were stitched upon both sides of the coat as decorations, into which the buttons of the opposite side could be fastened. It was a "double breaster," and, either buttoned or unbuttoned, presented a stunning effect and carried terror to me. I had a fear of this man of distinguished appearance, who looked like a *real professor*. He had been a teacher of penmanship in a large city and acquired there his superb style, while I was a mere boy, naturally timid, and destitute of a fine showing. That overcoat was a nightmare to me. How could I cope with such a man and such a coat! When I came to see his work my fear diminished, for even to my inexperienced eye it was clearly inferior. Professor Brightly kept me cheered with praises and I was sanguine, yet always eager for more instructions. He was touring the smaller towns and I was left much alone, and availed myself of chances for more knowledge. When I found a man who had a superior point in his work I secured it. In the first two years of my practice I repeatedly paid for methods and processes from those in advance of me, considering it better policy than digging it out myself, for the present use and advantage had a real value. A man named Lawyer, who had been operator for Meade Brothers, in New York city, showed me work of such excellence that I employed him to stop and teach me. Mr. Lawyer had a hobby. It was a *moist buff*, his theory being that moisture in a buff for polishing plates gave a deeper and richer polish than could otherwise be attained, and the deeply polished plate gave a finer image. Under his instructions I had a number of buffs and kept one or more down cellar when not in use, and changed them as required. The little moisture absorbed by the buckskin from the damp atmosphere did give a fine polish and the plates so polished gave fine pictures. I thought his instructions good and was well pleased that I had employed him.

Now came Professor Powelson, carrying an air of intelligence and success. His work was fine, yet differing in a way from Mr. Lawyer's, and because it differed I coveted it, and so took instructions from him. He, too, had a hobby. He showed me that the foundation for fine daguerreotype work was a finely polished plate, which could only be secured by a *perfectly dry buff* of fine buckskin well rouged, and the finishing touch given with calcined lampblack upon another buff of buckskin thoroughly dried.

The Powelson method necessitated a special drying-box slightly heated by a spirit lamp burning under a funnel-shaped tube of tin running up through the box. The dry buff produced a fine polish and excellent work; the opposite methods were both good, so I was content to know them both.

I had been much troubled at first on account of the shirt bosoms and other parts which should have taken white in the picture, but came out blue. I did not like it and asked my first instructor why it was and how to prevent it. He explained that it was bad indigo put into the starch, preparatory to ironing the shirt, and the reflection from it blued the surrounding parts. Since we did not always get blue linen, it might be inferred that all samples of indigo were not bad. A visiting daguerre-otypist making a friendly call referred to it as a blemish in my work. I asked him if he knew a remedy for it. He

Frank G. Schumacher, Photographer, Los Angeles, Cal.

GOING TO THE PARTY.

said, " Oh, yes, but I shall want $10 for it." I agreed to pay his price if the remedy proved successful. He told me to slightly increase the blaze of my spirit lamp under my mercury bath and try a picture. This I did, and my trouble in that respect was gone. I not only got white linen, but secured a richness of tone I had not before, so I was pleased with my investment. The man earned his $10 easily, but it was an advantage to me worth more than I paid. Thus I got my education. Many men had secrets to sell and I was a ready buyer, as it seemed my only course for advancement. A few months later, one very wet day there came into our studio a very wet man. He said he was a daguerreotypist, had missed his boat, and came in for a friendly call. He handed me his card which read:

CHARLES E. JOHNSON,
CLEVELAND, OHIO.

He was just from New York, and on his way home to Cleveland, where he had a business of his own. He said he had formerly been operator for Plumb, of New York, and that he had a daguerreotype of his daughter and her babe — possibly I would like to see it. He showed it me, and I was fairly dazed with the beauty of it. I had seen nothing before to approach it, nor dreamed a thing could be so beautiful. The lady was loveliness itself; the child was a miniature edition of her, sitting upon a little table leaning its baby cheek against the mother's. The position and every detail of arrangement was perfect. Beaming from the mother's face was a flood of love for the baby. The superior quality of texture, tone, color, coloring and finish was quite beyond my ability to describe. I had never before had such a pleasure in a picture. Finally he handed me another picture, a view of Superior street, the principal business thoroughfare of his city. It was beautifully taken and showed a fine street. In the immediate foreground of this view was a heavy post extending up from the sidewalk, with a large washbowl and pitcher on top, marking O. A. Brooks's crockery store, a landmark remembered by old Clevelanders of half a century ago. I told him I had never before seen anything so fine, and was sure I could never equal it. He said, " Oh, yes, it will be easy enough when you know how, and I can easily teach you." He told me that quality of work resulted from a discovery of his own — he had made a modification in the chemicals employed, using a " dry quick " instead of the usual " liquid quick " in common use. The

FAMILY GROUP — TAKEN IN 1850.

price was $15. He said he had sold the formula to the leading
proprietors in New York city, and all were glad to get it. The
opportunity for securing such a prize could not be missed. I surely
must have it, and said, " Yes, I will take it." The formula for
this " quick " was the mixture of German bromine with air-slacked
lime, to saturation, the older the lime the better. I was to send to
Dr. J. R. Chilton, chemist, New York city, for the bromine, " mind
you, German bromine," said Mr. Johnson, as I paid him. " Now,
good-by, young man; I wish you success. If you ever come to
Cleveland, give me a call. I shall be glad to see you," and he was
gone. My heart was " all a-flutter " in my new possession. Now
Voigtländer and I were better prepared to face the world. The
following morning I commenced the hunt for air-slacked lime. I
had the great luck to find, in the possession of a friend, a kegful

which had been in his attic three years, and it soon was mine. I had sent for the bromine the night before. When it came I commenced at once the preparation. In a wide-mouth ground-stoppered bottle of good size I put a quart of the lime and introduced the bromine a little at a time, as directed, shaking thoroughly between each addition until the fumes of the bromine were absorbed in the lime. At last I was ready. I had secured a special coating-box for the new "quick," and I made a trial — in fact, I made repeated trials — and it worked, and worked well, though not giving results equaling the finished samples I had seen and hoped for. I was a bit disappointed, but I tried to comfort myself that I must not expect everything at once. It must be worked out. I found on continued use of my dry quick it was really a great advantage, and so was content with my investment.

Occasionally the Professor showed up. He was more interested in lecturing and selling phrenological charts than in making daguerreotypes, so his tours were extended to greater distances. He had gotten new trousers, of better length, had discarded rubbers for daily wear, blackened his boots, and was really getting quite smart. He was desirous of selling out. I was inclined also to go out for myself, but at his desire I took charge of the business for a share of the proceeds as compensation.

Now came the announcement of the discovery of gold in California, which had a favorable effect upon our business. The country was all astir for a time, as the "California fever" raged intensely. Young men with golden visions were going, fathers mortgaged their property to raise money for their sons, while many forgot their years and went out with the boys. There had been nothing in the history of the country to so excite and interest the people, and on every hand great preparations were being made, while the "overland" and the "voyage by sea" were discussed by everybody. Parties of friends clubbed together to do or die, or to get gold. The perils of the journey were little understood. The unknown route, the danger from hostile Indians, the chance of perishing from illness or starvation; of leaving bleached bones upon the plains, were chances to be taken and to be considered before starting. There was much of heroism to be exercised — on the one side sure privation and hard experiences; on the other hand, possible success. *Gold, gold,* some gold, or a lot of gold! So they take their lives in their hands and start. Before leaving on this desperate enterprise, daguerreotypes were wanted to leave

George W. DeVore, Photographer, Leamington, Canada.
A CHIEF OF THE CHIPPEWAS.

with friends, and it gave me work.   Many who came for likenesses brought with them outfits to be shown in their pictures.   Tents, blankets, frying pans in which to cook bear meat, buffalo steaks and smaller game by the way, and to wash out their gold on reaching the diggings.   Among the explorers was young Billy Randolph, a jeweler's clerk, a modest boy fair enough to have been a girl, and many a girl could envy him his pure complexion and fine color. He was indeed a beautiful boy and the idea of *his* going out to " rough it " with brawny men seemed almost a pity, but a stout heart and plucky spirit lived under Billy's shirt.   He went out

with the boys and men, made his mark and his pile.   I shall never
forget him.   He paid me the first money I ever received — my
very own — for a daguerreotype.   It was a two-and-a-half-dollar
gold piece.   For many years I have found much fault with myself
for failing to keep that coin; but I did not stop to think or realize
at that time, how highly I would value it, did I possess it now.
Ah, Billy!   Playfellow, schoolmate, comrade!   Never again can I
see you.   'Tis said the streets are paved with gold where you have
gone; may you have a good claim staked off there!   But the little
golden coin you gave me was from unknown diggings, and can only
be known to me as a memory through all my life.

A spirit of unrest possessed me, a natural diffidence and lack
of confidence in myself was my bane.   I was always fancying that
people who had known me as a boy about the streets, only a few
years back, were seeing the absurdity of my claim to being a
daguerreotypist.   I had heard " a prophet was without honor in his
own country," and so concluded to go elsewhere.   Therefore I advised the Professor that I must be relieved of my engagement, as I
was bent upon going out for myself.   The companionship between
Voigtländer and myself was congenial and comfortable.   We
would go out together and see what fortune had to say to us.
Although settled upon going, it was a matter of some days' consideration before I could determine where.   I was timid about
trying at first any considerable town or village, and decided upon
going into the country among the farmers, where I had some
acquaintance.   I had been, as a boy, employed by Deacon Lyon, a
rich fruit grower who marketed his crops in Ithaca, and, during
the ripening season, drove in two and three times a week with the
product of his orchards.   I made overtures to him for a visit to the
farm, with a view to doing a little business among his neighbors in
likenesses.   He was quite pleased to have me go.   It was something of a novelty to have a daguerreotype man at one's house.
He had some daughters and a son at home who would surely be
pleased, and he was quite agreeable to it as well.   When within a
couple of miles of home, he called out to his neighbors in passing,
that for a few days he was going to have a daguerrean artist at his
house, and if they wished to have likenesses taken they would have
a chance.   At all events they were invited to come up and see the
folks, and the pictures.   It was more than I expected of the deacon,
but I was glad to be announced and advertised by him.   At one
house he drove up and waited for " the folks " to come out.   There

I was introduced to the mother and daughter of the house, and the announcement was again made that pictures would be taken at his house for a few days, and the invitation extended for them to come up. There was a broad veranda extending across the front of the spacious home of Deacon Lyon. Upon this the trunk containing my gallery outfit was placed, and quite a flurry of interest it developed when Mrs. Lyon and her two young lady daughters learned what it meant. Upon this veranda I con-

P. S. Ryder, Photographer, Syracuse, N. Y.

THE DEBUTANTE.

cluded to take my pictures. The large trees in front proved a good protection from the too strong light, and softened it to my liking. When, on the following morning, the deacon was about to start for town with his load of fine peaches, showing temptingly in the well-filled baskets, I asked to be allowed to "take" him and his load before tying the covering over the fruit. I objected to his putting on his better coat and hat, and took him as he was, as the farmer market man. It was a hit. That picture went over the neighborhood, was seen and admired by a dozen families, and many came to the deacon's to see it. I took quite a number of pictures on the deacon's porch, and was invited to move to other farmhouses and take members of the families. I was kept busy in this work among farm people for some weeks. The district in which I operated was a rich and prosperous one. All were "well-to-do farmers" and could easily afford to spend a few dollars for family likenesses. I began to feel the pleasure of prosperity for myself. The consciousness of carrying in my pocket more dollars than I had ever done, or counted upon, was a splendid gratification Invitations to visit new localities were extended in good time to prevent my taking trouble about where next? It was pleasant to be in demand. There had been two calls for me to go to "the village," a quiet little center some five miles distant. I concluded I was by this time sufficiently experienced to venture upon higher ground, so resolved to take the plunge from farms to a real metropolis. There was no hotel in the village. There was a main street and a cross street, a store and postoffice, a grist mill and sawmill, driven by a passing stream. In addition to the above was a wagon shop and a blacksmith shop. These comprised the business traffic and industries of the center. The prominent lady of the place, whose husband was merchant and postmaster, welcomed me to her home and permitted me to use her parlor, the finest in the village, in which to make my sittings, rent free. My sleeping room, the best in the house, and board, cost me two dollars per week. My little frame of specimen pictures was hung upon the picket fence beside the gate. When my camera was set up, the clip headrest screwed to the back of a chair, and background and reflecting screen tacked upon frames, I was ready for business. I used the open front door for my light. I could ask for nothing better. It was really surprising the interest that was manifested. People came in throngs, and from miles away. Mine was the first camera in the village and it created a sensation. I was busy with customers all the days. The dollars rolled in right merrily; no business in town equaled mine. The good lady of the house was the possessor of a large cluster breastpin which was lent to every female sitter, to the mutual satisfaction of lady owner and lady sitter. It was also a great aid to me, proving a capital point for aiming my focus. After the day's work a saunter across the bridge and through the path of the meadow, where the pleasant perfume of clover and the glad ripple of the brook greeted me, was my pleasure and my habit. The home-coming farmer gave me pleasant greeting. The boy with torn hat and trousers rolled half way to the knee, as he fetched the cows from pasture, hailed me with "Take my likeness, mister?" The village lasses,

Louis F. Jansen, Photographer, Buffalo, N. Y.

A FRENCH CHARACTER.

shy and sweet, gave modest bows, as they met the " likeness man."
I was regarded with respect and courtesy. All were friendly and
genial. All save one. The blacksmith, a burly man, the muscular
terror of the village, disapproved of me — said I was a lazy dog,
too lazy to do honest, hard work, was humbugging and swindling
the people of their hard earnings. He, for one, was ready to help
drive me out of the village. The greater my success, the more
bitter his spleen. In the abundance of his candor he denounced
me to my face as a humbug, too lazy to earn an honest living, and
said he wouldn't allow me to take his dog; that I ought to be
ashamed to be robbing poor people. Other uncomplimentary
things he said which were hard to bear, but in view of his heavy
muscles and my tender years I did not attempt to resent. Well!
I left the little village and the brawny blacksmith one day and
moved to another town some miles distant. A week later I was
greatly surprised by a visit from him; he had driven over to the
new place to find me. He had a crazed manner which I did not
understand and which filled me with terror. He demanded that I
put my " machine " in his wagon and go with him — straight, at
once. I asked why he desired it, and what was the matter. Then
the powerful man burst into a passion of weeping quite uncon-
trollable. When he could speak he grasped my hand, and through
his tears told me his little boy had been drowned in the mill-race
and I must go and take his likeness. " A fellow-feeling makes us
wondrous kind." My sympathy for the poor fellow in his wild
bereavement developed in me a tenderness for him which brought
him closer to me than any friend I had made in the village. I am
not ashamed to say I could not keep tears back from my own eyes.
All the way back to the village he wept and moaned — " My boy,
my boy!" I am glad to say I was fortunate in getting a good
picture of the little fellow. I never saw a man more grateful or
more repentant than was that poor blacksmith. From that time
he was my devoted friend. He came repeatedly to visit me, always
bringing with him the picture I had taken, and had a desire to
show it to me again and again. He insisted that I go home with him
for over Sunday, which I did. He wanted to erase the blemish of
his unfair treatment of me, and I did all I could to show him he had
succeeded.

CHAPTER III.

QUILTING-BEE.

For some months I drifted about and at length got into northern Pennsylvania. At one small town the landlady of the hotel
where I was stopping asked me one morning if I could not use
some other room than the ball-room for the following day, as the
ladies of the church were going to have a " quilting " and there was
no other available room in the village where two sets of frames
could be set up. The quilting was to be followed by a dance in the
evening. Of course I was very willing to vacate the room for the
ladies, and so told Mrs. Jenks. For the benefit of city people who
buy quilts and comfortables at stores, who have never made quilts
or seen them made, I will explain. Quilting frames were formed
of four wooden pieces about eight feet long four inches wide, and
perforated with holes every eight or ten inches, through which
wooden pegs or large nails are pushed to hold them together when
set up for use. Along the entire length of the frames is tacked
listing (the marginal edge of heavy wool cloth), to which the sides
and ends of the quilt are sewed when made ready for the quilting.
When not in use these frames are usually kept away upstairs, out
of the way. It was not considered necessary for all families to
possess these frames, but it was expected that owners would lend
them, and so a set would do for a neighborhood. As an extra set
was wanted for this occasion, Mrs. Jenks sent her son over to the
Wilkinses for theirs. Mr. Wilkins failed to tie the ends together,
but just balanced them upon Henry's shoulder; told him he should
carry them steadily and he would get along all right, then started
him off. Any boy who has carried quilting frames upon his shoulder knows their tendency is to slip — generally forward, and they
are also liable to spread apart at the ends. Henry's efforts to keep
them well bunched and balanced were not successful, for the ends
would spread apart, and they would slip endwise. He tried to
hold them together by leaning his head over upon them; the sharp
edges hurt his ear, and brought mutterings of bad words from him.
In his impatience he pitched them off in the road and kicked them,

using meanwhile very objectionable language. He tried again, and after several repetitions of loading and unloading finally reached home and slammed them down upon the porch with such violence as to bring his mother out with the exclamation, "Why Henry! My son, what's the matter?" Henry replied in a voice bursting with rage, "I'm going to run away and go to sea — that's what's the matter! No more carrying dod dummed slippery quilting frames for me." A few minutes later Henry was seen with a piece of pie so large it took both hands to keep it from breaking apart; and bites out of it, surprisingly wide and deep, certified to the abatement of his anger. Into the ball-room were now brought eight chairs, which were placed six or seven feet apart with the back of each chair toward the center of the room, and upon the backs of these chairs were placed the quilting frames, the holes adjusted, and the heavy nails pushed through, thus holding them together. The two sets of frames being set far enough apart to admit of two women to sit at each end and each side, the room began to assume an air of business. While a part of these good women sewed the bottom or wrong side of the quilt to the listings and spread the cotton batting evenly over it, others were engaged in preparing the blocks which formed the pattern and right side. "Oh! what pretty blocks," said Mrs. Cummings, as Mrs. Ruggles spread out some squares.

"Yes, I think them be rather pretty. My Melissa done them of evenings last winter, besides cutting and sewing carpet rags for our sitting-room. Melissa is a powerful smart girl, if I do say it as shouldn't say it. See how nice she has jined them diamond pieces, the stitches done as even as machine could do it. You notice that red and white piece? Well, that is a piece of my little Amy's dress who died when she was only four. And this is a piece that the minister's wife give me — the minister that was here before this one. Here's a piece of my mother's wedding dress. I've kept it laid away all these years; this is a piece of dress I wore when Ruggles come a-sparking me. Oh yes, they're ready to baste it onto the lining now, but I'll tell you more about it when we've got it off the frames, and hemmed." "I see you've got some new neighbors, the Sayles. Be they our kind of folks?" "Well," said Mrs. Cummings, "I don't know them much, they've sent over twice for a drawing of tea, and they've borrowed our brass kettle and ain't returned any on 'em yet." "Well, I swan!" said Mrs. Ruggles, and continued, "I 'spect you know the Joneses. They

F. G. Schumacher, Photographer, Los Angeles. Cal.

YOUNG ARISTOCRATS.

ain't much! There's their boy Bill, he don't know enough to come
in when it rains. You know he had the imperence to come to see
Melissa, but she give him his walking papers pretty sudden.
They're poor as skimmed milk, but they must keep five dogs,
besides all their young ones. Let a circus come to town and by
hook or by crook they must all go. I'll bet a cookey they'll get
their dogereytypes taken now this new man has just come, and
next winter we'll have to put in and help to keep them out of the
poorhouse; but some pork will boil so. Now, Miss Cummings, as
you ain't lived here very long and don't know folks very well, I
want you to be careful what you say to that Miss Higgins. She's
a regular tattler and makes more mischief than any three wimmin
in town, *but for all the world don't tell her I said so.* Why! here
she comes now! Why! howde do, Miss Higgins. I'm so glad to
see you. How's Mr. Higgins and the children? I didn't see you
to meeting last Sunday? Miss Higgins, this is Miss Cummings.

She's lately come to the village.   Almost a stranger yet, I'm sure
you'll like her first-rate, she's come from out west, she's a widder.
I want you and her to come and take a cup of tea with me soon's
you can find it handy, and we'll get better acquainted.   Mebbe
Mr. Hunter will come, his wife died last fall and the poor man is
very lonesome.   Why here! I see you wimmin are all started.
Just bite me off a long needleful of thread, Miss Jenks, and pass it
over.   I ain't going to let nobody outquilt me.   Well! if here don't
come the minister hisself!   Why Mr. Goodman, you can't quilt.   I
s'pose you jist come to keep us wimmin out of mischief.   I heard
a lady of your congregation say you was the dearest man we ever
had here.   You can stay here all right, but you must be good and
not hender us."   " I should be very sorry, Sister Ruggles, to be a
hindrance to you.   I thought it would be friendly to look in upon
you, as I am interested in all church matters.   I must make my
call short.   I have more work to do upon my sermon for next Sabbath.   I'll bid you good morning."   " There! " said Mrs. Jenks,
" you've driven him off; you're always sticking your foot in it.
He wouldn't thought of going only for what you said."   " Well!
Miss Jenks, a body can express theirselves, can't they?   There's
no law agin it, is they?   I didn't say 'twas you said he was so sweet
and dear, did I?   That Chambers girl with red hair and cross eyes
is kinder settin' her cap at him.   She looks like a charge of bran
from a musket had been fired into her face, but I can tell you
there's something else 'sides ' nits and lice ' in *her* head.   You wake
up the wrong passenger if you take *her* for a fool.   The minister
says there's witchery in her eyes.   Well! I vum! if they aint got
their quilt off from that other frame!   You wimmin talk too much
here.   You can't talk and work.   I'll bet they's some long stitches
in that quilt — they've set out to beat us and I guess they have."
" Now ladies," says Mrs. Jenks, " As soon as we get this quilt off
we'll clear out the frames and the chairs and ' red up ' the room for
the dancing and then we'll go down stairs, drink a cup of tea and
have a bite of something to eat."

Mr. Jenks here appeared and announced to his wife that the
table was set, the tea ready and her company could come right
in — " from labor to refreshment."   " That, ladies," said Mrs. J.,
" is some of Jenks's lodge talk.   He's pretty full of it since he's
joined the Masons.   These Masons have ways of expressing theirselves that's very mysterious."   As the ladies filed in and took
seats at the table his wife said, " Now, Mr. J., you and the girl just

SISTER KATE IN 1849.

wait upon the ladies while I pour the tea. Miss Cummings, how
do you take your tea?" "With trimmings!" answered Mrs.
Cummings.

"How will you have yours, Miss Ruggles — with sweetening?"

"No, just plain, Miss Jenks. I like it so best — it rests a
body so."

At this juncture a side door to the dining-room opens a few
inches and the voice of Henry is heard: "Ma! save me some of the
custard!" "Why, Henry Jenks! I'm ashamed of you. Where's
your manners? Go, like a good boy, and find the dogeretipe man,
and have him come and take tea with us, 'stid of waiting for the
regular supper. He's good company, and I'm sure the ladies would
like him." Continuing she added: "Did you see the picture he
took of the Chambers girl? Her freckles didn't show hardly a bit

and he made her look real pretty, I do declare." " Mr. J., pass the cold meat to Miss Higgins, and pass the biscuits too. I don't know as they'll be fit to eat, I didn't have very good luck with them." " Why, Miss Jenks, what makes you say so?" exclaimed Mrs. Ruggles, " I think them just delicious, they're so light and tender; I wish I could make such good ones; with your nice butter and honey they just melt in a body's mouth. I must get your recipe for making them." The pride which animates the heart of a noted good cook at praise of her baking shone from the happy face of Mrs. Jenks, as she said, " Certainly. Miss Ruggles, you'll be very welcome." " I hear," said Mrs. Ruggles to Mr. Jenks, " that Thomas's dog has been killing some of your sheep." " Yes," said Mr. Jenks, " I seen Thomas an hour ago. I just went to work and told him I'd kill that dog soon as I laid eyes on him. He had the imperence to say I'd get in trouble if I teched that dog. Well, I took and told him I'd kill his dog and give him a licken' to boot, and he didn't dast to answer back." The side door opens again a little way and Henry calls out, " Ma, don't forget the pie; save some for me, ma!" Now Mrs. Jenks cuts a fine, large cake, and together with another plate of sliced cake they are passed to all; dishes of preserves are also passed and evidently enjoyed by all. Mrs. Ruggles' enthusiasm is expressed with vigor. " Miss Jenks, you are a born cook. This is very pretty eating. I never tasted such vittles before. If you wouldn't mind I'd like to take to Melissa just a little taste of this cake." " Certainly, with pleasure, Miss Ruggles. Let me fill up your cup, just to warm it up a little; I'm so glad you like my cake." "Why, Henry Jenks, where's your manners? I'm surprised," said Mrs. Jenks, as Henry burst in through the side door. " Well," said Henry, " I knowed you must be through by this time; I'm hungry as a dog. Couldn't wait another minute!" The ladies here withdrew, leaving the field clear to Henry. Mrs. Jenks now discovered seated in a list-bottom rocker in a bedroom just off the dining-room, Mrs. Pelton, a very quiet neighbor and member of the church, in whose interest the " bee " was given. " Why, sakes alive! Miss Pelton. You sitting here alone! You ain't been to the table nor had a mouthful to eat. What's the matter?" " Well," said Mrs. Pelton, " it's all my own fault. Fact is, I came away and forgot my teeth. I had them done up in a clean white rag, and 'stid of putting them in my pocket came off and left them in the stand drawer. Just like me. I'll forget my head next." At " early candle light " began to

F. Dundas Todd, Photographer, Chicago, Ill.

FOURSCORE AND FOUR.

arrive young men and maidens in dancing trim — "biled shirts"
and low pumps, the latter newly coated with white of egg to make
them sleek and shiny, for the young men; white dresses with a
blue or pink ribbon with ends fluttering around the waist, a flower
in the hair for the girls, anticipated pleasure beaming from their
faces.   They came from the farms for miles around, in buck-
boards and buggies, till the wagon shed was filled.   The parlor and
sitting-room below contained the "beauty and chivalry" of the
village, and around about.   Rosy cheeks and bright eyes which
were dancing in anticipation, witching glances, happy smiles, witty
flashes and repartee, charming coquetry and sweet blandishments;
girls looking good enough to eat, and young men looking hungry.
When from the dancing-hall came a sound of well-rosined bows
drawn across sensitive and resounding strings of fiddles harmoniz-
ing themselves to unison of tone for the revel soon to begin,
thrilled and vibrated every nerve and muscle like the touch of a
"funny-bone" shock, putting into the dancing muscles the witchery and delight which tingles from toe to finger end, and makes difficult to keep the feet still, or upon the floor.

There was a rush and scramble to that hall of pleasure, and the spluttering tallow candles revealed upon the dais platform Nate Adams, first fiddle; Joe Moon, second fiddle; Leb Wright, cello and master of ceremonies.

A march was struck up and the couples answered to it by stepping off promptly and in good order. When the march ended and the music ceased, the couples formed to places, Leb Wright "rose to the occasion," and said: " Now, young fellows and girls, there's going to be a dance. It's going to be right here, in this room; we fellows here are going to give you the music. You mustn't kick too high, or laugh too loud, because it's for the benefit of the church. We'll start with a cotillion. Now away you go! All hands around." And away they *did* go. Not boisterous, but with a spring and activity of ardor pleasant to see. Merry hearts and willing feet responded to the music, and the music led them through delightful turns, swings, and balances, as prescribed by the genial suggestions of director Wright. Occasionally in the more enthusiastic passages of sudden whirls of " swinging partners," the " swish " of female skirts and the " stand out " of the young men's coat tails was a breezy accompaniment to music strains and merry laughter. Miss Chambers was there! She was simply and modestly charming, without seeming to know it, and without a seeming thought of any one suspecting it — even herself. She was clearly a superior girl, and easily the belle of the party. Her manner was sweet and unobtrusive; even the girls liked to put an arm around her waist — yes, a girl on each side of her. She was a graceful dancer and much in demand. The minister thought there was " witchery " in her eyes, was Mrs. Ruggles' declaration. The minister was right — but it was a sweet and innocent witchery. Her smile was the sunshine of a June morning, her hair 18-K. gold, burnished in the lights and sobered gold in shadows. Gracious! But I wanted to take that girl's picture every time I saw her. I didn't blame her girl friends for putting an arm around her. I didn't blame the minister for seeing witchery in her eyes. I think I lost a piece of my heart that night. Of the young men present was one who seemed to me unlike the others — as though he was partially a stranger. The cut of his clothes showed a bit more style and his manners more polish. He was especially fine looking — had a little dash of the world about him, like he had been somewhere and seen something. He seemed well known to the company in general, was genial and courteous with all of both sexes, but a

D. D. Spellman, Photographer, Detroit, Mich.

THE VIOLINIST.

little more with Miss Chambers than the others. I learned he had once been a resident of the village, but had settled in a near-by city, had a wealthy father, had been through college, had graduated from a law school and had the world before him. On went the dance until well past midnight — happy and joyous — every toe tingling with pleasure, every step enjoyed to the fullest. At last came " Money Musk," the recognized wind-up of the program. Leb Wright rose again and said: " Now, young ladies and young fellows, the hop is generally over at this point, but we have the pleasure of announcing for this evening only, a little exhibition of fancy dance by a couple you all know well. After the dance you'll find supper waiting for you in the Jenks' banquet hall. I will also announce that Joe Terrill, up on the ridge, gives a housewarming to his new hotel a week from to-night. Of course there'll be a bit of a shindy." Now the music starts again, and the future Francis Granger, the modest lion of the evening, escorts Miss Chambers to the center of the ball-room, when slowly and gracefully commences a waltz by this charming couple. The sweet poetry of motion is portrayed smoothly and deliciously; gradually it increases in ardor and interest, it grows in intensity, reaching almost a point of delirium. The music changes to schottish, to polka, and is followed by the dancers to a fury of dashes and plunges until the exhibition was over and the luxuries of the table were sought.

I retired to my bed to dream of witching eyes and golden hair.

Miss Belle Johnson, Photographer, Monroe City, Mo.

FOUR OF A KIND.

CHAPTER IV.

JEDUTH GRAVES.

A few days after the dance, Mr. Jenks introduced me to a man who had come to his hotel on business relating to an estate in which they were both interested. His name was Graves. He was a cousin to Jenks, and he was also a tavern-keeper in the adjoining county, on the other side of the mountains. He took a fancy to me at once and wanted me to go home with him. He said no one had ever been there taking likenesses and he thought I could do well. At least I could have a good time — plenty of young people, socially inclined, and the older class genial and hospitable. Great trouting, over there; the brooks so full they crowd each other. " I'll take a day off and show you around. Come! What say, young fellow?" I told him I was " as wax in his hands;" that I would follow wherever he led. " Now, that's the stuff, young fellow," said Mr. Graves. " I keep a strictly temperance house. No drunkards made or harbored about my premises." Having no inclination for indulgences of a barroom character, I was well pleased, and wondered why he should gratuitously give me such information. Perceiving him to be agreeably eccentric, with a leaning to humor, I soon adjusted myself to his whimsicalities, and gave him good length of rope. His philosophy was to make the best of the world as it unfolded itself to him, and to never " cry over spilled milk." The stage which was to carry us over to his place was due at noon. I packed up and was ready for the stage-coach when it halted for dinner at the Jenks tavern. I bade good-bye to Mr. and Mrs. Jenks and Henry — whose capacity for custard pie I shall never forget — and away we started up the mountain. It was a slow, tedious pull to the summit, from whence it was down hill all the way to our destination. Mr. Graves shortened the distance with entertaining talk. His fancy for me was gratifying and complimentary. He treated me like an old friend, was confidential and affable, was ready to tell me everything about himself and willing to learn all I was inclined to tell him of myself. I soon learned his mother and his wife were the best of women —

his mother the very best in the world. That information was to me a guarantee of his own worth. He said he was born in the mountains of Pennsylvania and brought up as farm boys usually are — to work, and told me in serious confidence he did not like it. Farm life, he said, was too monotonous. He tired of seeing the same fields, the same plow and oxen, day after day, and wanted something more stirring. He thought he would like to be a peddler, a horse jockey, or a sailor. The adventurous spirit in him craved activity. After " some words " with his father one day he left the plow in the furrow and engaged in the wild life of a raftsman, took to floating logs down the river to supply the lumber market. The panoramic variety of rugged banks, rocky shores, through the woods, past green fields and occasional villages, past which the river carried him, made a pleasant change which he gladly welcomed. A long sweep oar at either end of the raft by which to steer and keep it from running into the shores was all the care necessary. There was no machinery to get out of order, no firing up or watching of steam gauge. To drift with the current was easy. To tie up at night against the river bank, a crew of two men could do. It was quite a jolly life. One memorable night, in a gale, he was swept from the deck and apparently drowned. He was found next morning upon the sands of the shore where he had been washed by the waves. Now this being Mr. Graves' story rather than my own, I step aside and let him tell it in his own words. " Well," said Graves, " as soon as it was noised about that a man was drowned and on exhibition, people gathered as quickly as though it had been a dog fight. As I never had been drowned before it was a new experience to me. I seemed to know I was in some way the attraction. I could hear, as through a fog, what was being said, but could not move or speak. Most all of them said ' poor fellow! ' One chap, who I thought must be a raftsman, said ' poor devil! ' One woman said, ' I wonder if he had a wife and children,' then burst out crying. A man said, ' He's not lying comfortable; you fellows lift him by the shoulders and I'll swing his legs around.' Another asked, ' Don't any one know this man? ' The answer was, ' No, he's a stranger; probably from up river somewhere ' Another spoke, saying, ' Poor fellow, his troubles are over. We've all got to go that way sooner or later.' A woman said, ' God save me! but I've seen that man before. He's Jeduth Graves, from Great Bend.' Recognizing the name and reviving, I said, ' Right you are, madame.' It is so unusual to hear a drowned

A. J. Swanson, Photographer, Faribault, Minn.

"OH, FOR A WIFE!"

man talk the crowd rushed away in a panic. Well, sir,'' said Graves, '' that woman hustled for a carriage, loaded me in, took me to her hotel, nursed me back to life, and I married her. Quite romantic, wasn't it? She was a widow and owned the hotel. It was a case of love at first sight. You've heard of such things, I expect. We seem to have been just made for each other, and for the hotel business. We just run that house to the queen's taste.'' This latter declaration I found to be true. On arriving at the hotel he introduced me to Mrs. Graves, who was a comely woman and a typical landlady of that period. She made me comfortable at once, taking me about the house to the various rooms, that I might find my choice. When properly situated the ballroom offered the best light and I selected it here. On exhibiting my specimen pictures I invariably secured the interest of those who saw them. The newness of the art and the curiosity of most people inclined them to be interested. One particular daguerreotype I had seemed to capture every one who saw it. It was a picture of one of Dan Rice's circus wagons. I showed it to Mr. Graves as I was unpacking. He was quite pleased with it and borrowed it to show to his wife. The first time I went into the dining-room was for supper the evening of my arrival. The table was filled with a goodly number of guests, who seemed regular boarders. Mr. Graves was seated at the head of the table and placed me at his right. He gave me a rather unique introduction. He said: '' This young fellow is a likeness man. He's going to stay with us for a spell and give you a chance to have your likenesses taken.'' He then started the Dan Rice picture down the table on one side and it came back on the other, every one examining it with apparent interest. Mr. Graves then said, '' That name of Dan Rice on the wagon is the most natural thing I ever saw.'' Myself and my business were advertised from that minute. During the evening I busied myself unpacking and putting things in shape for business. About eight o'clock Mr. Graves came in and said, '' Young fellow, I think it time to knock off and call it a full day. Just come down stairs. I want to see you in my private office.'' I followed him down stairs through the general business and reading room, where he unlocked a side room into which he passed. He took the key from the lock, inserted it in the inner side, locking us in. He pointed to an arm chair on one side of a table, which I took, and he seated himself in the other, on the opposite side. Said Mr. Graves: '' Hot or cold?'' I did not understand. I was a little disconcerted at being locked in. He

Louis Fleckenstein, Photographer, Faribault. Minn.

HITTING TWO NAILS ON THE HEAD.

got up from his chair, opened an inner door near the corner of the room where I saw shelves, from which he took and placed upon the table a spirit lamp, a little metal stand and a small kettle, which I inferred was for heating water, two fine-looking tankards, with hinged metal covers, two drinking glasses and a decanter with something in it. I could no longer misunderstand. " Prefer it hot, I suppose," says Graves. " Why, Mr. Graves, you told me you kept a strictly temperance house." " Well, so I do, young fellow. Never sold a drop, but sometimes for sociability — did I understand you, hot?" " Yes, Mr. Graves, and to better acquaintance." While the water was heating Graves continued: " I abominate a sot. I will not harbor drinking men. I wouldn't have a bar in my house, but in my private office I sometimes like to sit with a friend — if I like him well. Now there's Father O'Halleran, as kindly a man as you could find, occasionally spends a half hour with me. He told me the other evening how he saved a man's life. A dissolute bum sort of fellow was telling a hard-luck story. Hadn't tasted food or had a drink for some hours; wanted a little help. The father took from his pocket a silver dollar and said, ' What would you do if I gave you that? ' ' I'd drop dead,' said the bum. The father said, ' I put the coin back in my pocket and saved the poor fellow's life,' adding, as he sipped his glass, ' Graves, you got a good brew on this.' " Without claiming to be expert in " savors " and " odors," I am impressed with the insinuating quality of a " hot Scotch," especially two, one on either side of a solid, thick, smooth surfaced, time-colored table. The ingredients and construction play a considerable part as factors. Jeduthan Graves certainly possessed a master hand and well-balanced eye for proportion. A thin glass, a dallying sip, lingeringly enjoyed, the grateful fumes rising to the nostrils — brainward — while the soothing liquid seems to find the heart, makes a fellow forget his enemies and believe 'tis a good world after all.

Through the vapory combination of tankard and cigars Mr. Graves found inspiration for spinning and weaving. A reminiscent wave swept over him. He delighted in his boyhood and his mother, who was mother and chum. He could always go to her for counsel, advice and sympathy. She seemed to understand the boy-nature better than his father did. She thought it better to lead his mind by gentleness than to obstruct it without giving a reason or explanation. " Mother was a religious woman," he said, " and took me to meeting with her. Preaching was held in a log school-

W. E. Vilmer, Photographer, Crown Point, Ind.

THE WHITE SQUAD.

house up in the mountains among the trees, where it was very
pleasant. Some folks came five or six miles and there were always
a number of horses tied to the trees. I got acquainted with some
boys and some of them carried in their pockets cookies to eat at
intermission, for we held two services. Mother put caraway seeds
in mine and the boys liked them better than their own, and I traded
with them. Mother liked to hold my hand in hers, even in meeting,
and sometimes it would get so sweaty she would wipe it upon her
handkerchief, and days when it was real warm I would sometimes
fall asleep and she would wipe my forehead. I didn't like to have
my hand held all the time, but I didn't want to tell her so, and
since she died I'm glad I didn't. Mother would have liked me to
be a preacher, but I really couldn't do it. I used to try to practice
after I had gone to bed at night, but the words wouldn't come to
me, and I would fall asleep. After her death I grew up to be a
sort of careless fellow, but I remember always how good she was;
she told me I must always say my prayers, and I always do. I
have thought it is not rigidly practiced by tavern-keepers, but I do

my share honestly. I know where she has gone and I count on hunting her up when I go ' over there.' " He said a good mother was the best thing that could happen to a man. " I can generally tell whether a man is ' O. K.' or ' N. G.' " said Mr. Graves. " I'd rather think a man was a good fellow or had good in him than be in doubt about it. Prejudice against people or things should not be encouraged; there's a good deal in breaking it down. A man that goes around with a scowl on his face and a chip on his shoulder is generally an unhappy cuss. He's quarreling with the world without just knowing it. I learned a lesson when a boy about overcoming prejudice that I have never forgotten. Now a man can learn from dumb beasts — mighty good lessons. I'd rather see the wag of a dog's tail than the glitter of his teeth. There's as much difference in men as there is in dogs. But I was saying what I learned about overcoming prejudice. Now you would hardly expect a cow to teach a man — but listen. Father had a valuable cow that had been ailing for some time and he was quite concerned about her. Mother said, one day, ' a good, big dose of soft soap is what she wants.' Father laughed a sort of incredulous laugh that had a tinge of pity in it for mother's ignorance, and said, ' Oh, pshaw! A cow take a dose of soft soap! You never could fool ' Old Moll ' — she wouldn't touch it.' ' Well, Daniel Graves,' said mother, ' I'll show you that you don't know all about cows.' So she took a good-sized feed bucket and two quarts of soft soap in a basin, she mixed in the bucket a mess of rich slops of bran and corn-meal, then added the two quarts of soft soap, stirred it thoroughly in and sprinkled a little salt over the top of the mixture. I watched interestedly the whole performance, being doubtful as to whether or not ' Old Moll ' would take her medicine, yet hopeful she would, so mother might win. Father carried the bucket out in the yard and placed it as a temptation to good ' Moll,' who at once plunged her nose quite to the bottom, then quickly withdrew, shaking her head and twisting her nose to an expression of loathing and a shudder of disgust, trying to drool the hateful dose from her mouth. For several minutes she stood and hated it. She resented it as an indignity unfairly put upon a worthy and faithful servant. Now, after waiting a time, carefully reached her tongue out, and, little by little, licked the bitter stuff off her nose and chops, as far as she could reach. What was beyond she wiped off on to her fore leg, then licked it cautiously into her mouth. Her prejudice against the stuff was very marked. She looked at the bucket,

Evan D. Evans, Photographer, Ithaca, N. Y.

OUT FOR QUAIL.

smelled of it, sniffed at it, and finally wiped her tongue into it, shuddered with a less intense disgust than before, but still hating it. Now, at a shorter interval, with feebler resistance, she dipped again, with a seeming ability to tolerate more heroically. An hour consumed in hating the soap and loving the meal, she finally emptied the entire contents of the bucket into her stomach. The sharp angle where the joining of the bottom and side staves met, where possibly a fine streak of the delicacy — for it was no longer a medicine — had been forced, ' bossy ' reached with her tongue and wiped over and over to secure the last remaining morsel. That was a case of *prejudice overcome.* Next day good ' Moll ' was entirely well, and frisky. Mother said, ' didn't I tell you so,

Daniel?' And father walked off into the barn without striking back — without even pretending to hear her.'' Then Mr. Graves said, '' You must be tired, young fellow; it is time to go to bed. I believe in keeping good hours.''

The '' entertainment '' was put back into the closet. I never saw the '' private office '' again. The next morning, having gotten my camera set up ready for operating, I invited Mr. Graves to sit for me by way of testing my chemicals, which resulted in my getting a striking and characteristic likeness of him, which pleased him greatly. If, before, there had been a doubt of success in that town, the doubt was swept away in that sitting. I never saw a man more interested than was that self-same tavern-keeper. He wanted to see how it was done and I showed him carefully, step by step, every point and every stage of likeness taking. He was as pleased as a child. He carried that picture in his pocket constantly and showed it everywhere. He brought many people to me and quite insisted upon their having sittings. He was indeed a good help to me and secured me much business, yet did not neglect his own in the meantime, but '' kept tavern '' all the time just the same. He always addressed me as '' young fellow,'' and spoke of me to others as the '' likeness man.'' He gave it out confidentially among his friends that I was the inventor of the art. He said to one of his friends, '' that young fellow studies most of the time. Just notice how big and thick his head is. That comes of hard study. Why, the room he occupies smells mysterious, and his camera is a wonderful little machine. A fellow that can make likenesses so true as he does of course has to have a good head on him.'' Sometimes early in the morning he would awaken me and say, '' It's a good morning for trout; they'll bite like wolves today. Hurry up and we will have a trout breakfast.'' We would start out at a sharp pace for a stream which was a little way from the village and in the edge of the wood, overshadowed by trees. As we neared the stream Mr. Graves cautioned me to silence, and to avoid noise in walking, '' For,'' said he, '' these little rascals are shy and suspicious to a fault. When they get a notion you are after them there's no doing anything with them. Just below here where there's an elbow in the stream, and a clump of bushes on the shore, is the spot to fill a small basket in short order.'' The small basket, with the bottom covered with fresh, green grass, was a part of our outfit and did not have to wait long for the beautiful speckled fellows from the cold, clear brook. Mr. Graves was

John Rösch, Photographer, White Plains, N. Y.

THE CHEF.

expert and I quite amateurish. He would drop three or four in the basket to my one. The joy I found in the few I caught kept me from discontent at his greater success. I had the grand satisfaction, our first morning out, of landing the biggest one in our basket. We were permitted to see Mrs. Graves manipulate the " little innocents," on flourboard, in frying-pan, thence to platter and upon the table. We recognize the weakness of words to describe the flavor of a fine group of those little chaps — just fresh caught — *by the man who eats them*. We extend sympathy to him who, from any chance, has not been privileged to *catch his trout* and *eat his trout*. If it should occur to him that in some small way life had failed to reach a climax, possibly he has been defrauded of a lively brook trout. Mr. Graves kept his word as to giving me a good time and a good business. I was six weeks in his town and carried away a fine pocketbook. My departure from that pleasant and profitable place was under protest of Graves. He said, " If you don't find it to suit you in Ohio, young fellow, come back here; we will take good care of you." All through the fifty odd years since I parted from Mr. Graves his image has lived in my mind. I have never seen his like since. I have never met a more companionable or peculiarly eccentric man. I have cheated myself of a pleasure in failing to go back and visit him. I often wonder if the streams swarm with trout as they did then. I wonder if he still keeps the tavern.

By courtesy of " Photographic Times-Bulletin."

" WHO SAID POSSOM ? "

CHAPTER V.

MY START FOR OHIO.

Having seen a fine daguerreotype, and that to have another look at it should pull a young enthusiast through three states may appear strange, I will admit; but it was the only way to satisfy a longing, and I yielded to it. I had not forgotten Mr. Johnson and his invitation to visit him if I ever went to Cleveland. I had not forgotten the beauty of the work he had shown me, it had lived in my mind as an ideal I hoped to attain. I cherished a hope that I might some day, through supreme effort and patience, find in my own work a semblance to his. I used to think if I could sweep the floors of his studio I would cheerfully do it for the privilege of seeing him work, and working with him.

Yes; I was headed for Ohio, and ultimately for Cleveland, bent upon further instructions from Mr. Johnson.

From the car windows as we went rushing through the country in its early spring dress of tender green and young shrubs, I was delighted with the valley of the Susquehanna, and the sweeps we made in rounding the curves of that beautiful river, presenting to view a new picture every few seconds, which was scarcely seen before another burst into view more striking in picturesqueness. Farms, homes and barns seemed to fly past us and out of sight rapidly. I was in a pleasant country, following the shores of a pleasant river, drinking in the beauties spread before us, enjoying every change of the rapidly growing and vanishing panorama.

While recognizing and enjoying the beauty of the scenery along the Susquehanna, my mind reached out in a grasping sense to Ohio, wondering if it could be anything like this. The comparison was soon dropped, for Ohio was a new country and could not yet presume to rival the Keystone state.

There were occasional instances of people emigrating from the neighborhood of my home in Central New York, to the western states. My boyish impressions were that in those new countries, or states, Ohio, Michigan and Illinois, those of which I heard most frequent mention, log houses, rail fences and stumps were the

usual thing through the country, and that they might occasionally
be seen in the villages and cities. In these earlier days the adventurous emigrants were people we had known among us, but whom
we were not likely to ever see again. Sometimes we would hear
that some one had received a letter from a friend who had moved
"away out West." The recipient was an envied person, and for a
time an important possessor of news. Neighbors would call to
inquire about these people who had moved almost out of the world;
and the letter would be read and shown again and again.

I knew of Sam Van Order, a citizen of my native village, who
had "moved his family West," and not liking the country had
returned. Sam's going was a matter of general interest. I had seen
the wagon in which he and his family explored the West. It was
covered with heavy awning cloth, held up by hoop-like arches fastened to each side of the high side-boards of the wagon, and at the
back drawn together by means of a heavy puckering string, leaving
a hole large enough to look through, like a back window.

Slung up by strong leather straps to the hoop arches inside,
was Sam's rifle. Under the seat of the wagon was a tool-box built
to the wagon, containing axe, saw, hammer, nails, strong cord,
etc. Cooking utensils, dishes, bedding and clothing such as were
necessary for the journey, were provided.

Crotched sticks and a parallel bar on which to hang pots and
kettles over the fire were a part of the outfit. Cooking and sleeping for some of the party were to be done outside the wagon. Many
friends were attracted by Sam's elaborate preparations and his
"gypsy wagon."

The day for departure came, the hearty good wishes of their
friends were given, and Sam's "prairie schooner" set sail.

For days and weeks they journeyed and drifted in search of a
satisfactory location; the fine districts he heard of and was directed
to were not to his liking. Finally, one morning, he determined to
resort to chance as to the direction to be taken, and told the family
of his resolve. His oldest son, Jim, whom Sam called "Chim" —
for Sam was a Dutchman of Pennsylvania type — was instructed
by his father to stand up a pole, which, when carefully balanced
was to be allowed to fall, and the direction in which it fell should
be the direction taken. After the pole was stood on end and properly poised Jim waited for the signal from his father, which came,
as follows: "Chim, lean de pole a leetle torge home! All right
now, Chim, let go." And they followed the pointer.

Louis Fleckenstein, Photographer, Faribault, Minn.

BOAT AHOY!

Here my thoughts take a new turn. I should pass through Ithaca and I determined to stop over. I knew that a gray-haired invalid woman would be sitting at her window, which commanded a view of the approach to her home. She would be watching out for me. She would meet me at the door. What a blessing to a young man is a good mother! He may go out in the world, being sure the mother's heart is always reaching out in tenderness and prayer for his safety and welfare. And now I was to be gone an indefinite period. I was going to a " far country " — to Ohio; which, to my dear mother, seemed the other side of the world, since it took her boy from her. The morning of my departure she gave me a parcel, hoping that in my traveling bag there would be room for it — begged me to be careful of myself; to write often; to not forget my home or my mother. There was Jonah Sinsibaugh at the door with his hack, and no time to lose — as he was a bit late. I made a rush for the hack, not daring to look back, and away we went for the boat which was to take me down the lake to meet the cars of the New York Central Railway. I took a look at the parcel when I got on board the boat. It contained a pair of mittens and a Bible — bless her dear old heart.

I was privileged to ride on " the new rapid steamer, *Simeon Dewitt*," with T. D. Wilcox, captain; " Alf " Goodrich, clerk; " Mart " Ryerson, pilot. She was a beauty, and Ithacans were proud of her. But for some years past she has been disrespectfully classed a " tub," and is probably pulled up in a side cove of the inlet for a marine cemetery, and doubtless some of her ribs are sticking up out of the weeds as monuments to her former greatness and as a mark to her last resting-place. Such is life — such is death. Peace to her remains.

The *Simeon Dewitt* visited the prominent places on the lake, dropping off and taking on passengers as she made her landings. She gave us a pleasant ride through the Cayuga, and landed us at the station of the Auburn & Rochester Railroad. We passed through Geneva, Canandaigua, Rochester, and arrived at Buffalo, where we took the steamboat *America* for Cleveland — no railroad west of Buffalo at that time. I was timid of making into Cleveland at once; had a feeling that I should skirmish about and get used to Ohio; so landed in the morning at Fairport, where the Grand river enters Lake Erie, distant from Painesville three miles, which was made by hack in time for breakfast at the Burridge House. Painesville was a beautiful village, and on the morning of my entrance was like a flower garden, or an orchard of peach blossoms, with which it abounded. It was the 25th of April, 1850, which, being my birthday, I have easily remembered. The Ohio I had found was so different from the Ohio I had expected to see, I was in a way disappointed. The towns and villages were as finished and up-to-date as the places I had been brought up in. Painesville was certainly a beautiful village; in my limited travels I had seen nothing finer. I looked about for a studio room and found a suitable one over the offices of the old Geauga Furnace Company, with P. P. Sandford as my landlord. The society of this proud little town was of a high standard, quite conservative and exclusive. My patronage came slowly, but surely. Here I met William H. Beard, the artist, a young man of remarkable talent, known later as the Landseer of America. His delight was in painting animals. He put souls in them; he humanized them; he dignified them. It was sometimes his pleasure to make wags of them, to make them frolic and rolicksome. A group of his tipsy bears, once seen, could never be forgotten. He glorified his subjects and glorified himself in the fame he made in painting them. He gave me his friendship; he opened my perception to a better understanding of art. My gratitude was kindled in those, my young days, and still burns faithfully.

F. R. Lockhart, Photographer, Toronto, Canada.

CHILDHOOD'S HAPPY HOURS.

CHAPTER VI.

THE KIRTLAND MORMON TEMPLE.

BOB BRIGGS,
of Painesville.

I had heard of the Mormon Temple at Kirtland, some ten miles from Painesville, had a curiosity to see it, and determined that should be my next stopping place. I bargained with Mr. Robert Briggs (familiarly known as Bob), a citizen of Painesville, who kept horses for hire, to haul me over. The price was a daguerreotype of himself and a silver dollar. When last I saw him he told me he still had the likeness, but had lost sight of the dollar.

The drive from Painesville to Mentor is as fine as can be found — straight, broad and level, fine farms on either side, orchards, broad fields with grazing cattle, well fed and sleek. The homes of the farmers were well kept, well painted and well fenced, showing thrift and prosperity. Shade trees were in abundance to protect and beautify; flowers and vines climbing over latticed porches, doors and windows; hollyhocks in rows and in many colors; sunflowers, poppies, marigolds and peonies. Old-fashioned flowers testified to the presence and good taste of the farm wives and daughters and the pride they took in tidy front yards and gardens; for be it known this superb road is a continuation of Euclid avenue, the pride of Cleveland, and famous as one of the most beautiful avenues in the world. Verily, on this delightful day the country through which we drove " had its face washed and its hair combed." Mr. Briggs entertained me with information as to the names of the residents and gave me gossipy sketches of their financial strength and moral standing. Not in a single instance did he report a blemish upon the character or good name of any resident. Really! is this Arcadia, or a road in Ohio? On reaching Mentor, we turned south, taking the road which leads to Kirtland, three miles distant. The flat evenness of the drive between Painesville and Mentor is changed as we proceed upon the crossroad, and

Wm. T. Higbee, Photographer, Cleveland, O.

CHUMS.

we find waves of undulation.   We are approaching a valley through
which runs a winding stream emptying in Grand River at Painesville, and by that route finds its way into Lake Erie.

As we approached the brow of the hill down which we were to go,
we stopped to admire the picturesque valley stretching to the east.
Before us was a winding road through overhanging trees leading
to the flats or lower part of the village. Kirtland flats comprise the
portion lying in the valley where was located the business of the
village, the store and postoffice kept by Mr. Isaac Sherman, a grist
mill, a wagon and blacksmith shop, and quite a number of scatter-
ing homes.   Kirtland on the hill represented more territory.   Over-
topping all were the Mormon Temple, a Young Ladies' Seminary,
once presided over by the late Gen. M. D. Leggett; the School for
Children, apart from the seminary, two taverns and a good number
of residences.

We drove down the hill under the arching trees, across the flats
and over the bridge.   Bob stopped at the watering trough, gave his
horses a drink, then commenced the ascent of the hill.   As we
reached the top the declining sun lighted up our side of the
temple, leaving the other in shadow, giving the building a bold and
striking effect against the sky for a background.   The shadows
from the spire fell upon Bump's Tavern, across the road.   We
drove over the shadow of the body without compunction or com-
ment.   A couple of young men were in front of the tavern
bantering for a horse trade as Bob and I drove up.   We were an
unusual arrival, with so large a piece of baggage as was necessary
to carry my daguerreotype outfit.

Sitting in front of that end of the tavern which contained the
barroom, and near the entrance door, were two men in chairs tilted
back upon the hind legs with the tops of the backs resting against
the side of the house, engaged in the pastime usual to loiterers
about taverns, of whittling.   Mr. Bump had been re-shingling the
wing of his house and some of the unused pieces made good material for the whittlers.   The chips from their work were scattered
about them upon the floor of the platform porch.   One of the men
knew Mr. Briggs, and as we dismounted from the low-box democrat
wagon he threw his chair forward and came out and helped to
unload my big trunk and place it in the hallway of the house.
" That fellow a peddler or a doctor? " he asked.   " There's a smell
of drugs and medicines in that trunk."   " No," said Briggs, " he's
a picture taker.   He's been taking likenesses down at Painesville

P. S. Ryder, Photographer. Syracuse, N. Y.

INTERESTED.

FIRST MORMON TEMPLE.

that looked like they could talk." "Say," continued Briggs, changing the subject, "do you know whether Cris Crary has sold them gray colts yet? Think I'll drive over and see him, now I'm so near."

Here Mr. Bump announced supper and we filed into the dining-room. There was a fair representation of people at table, among whom was Mrs. Bump, a kindly, motherly-looking woman, and their young daughter, a sweet child who made friends with me at once, and learning I was a likeness man invited me to "take her picture." I was well impressed with these genial people, and felt assured I would be well fed, judging from the generous table and good cookery. I may remark, a young man not long from his mother's ways of "dishing up things" recognizes and welcomes similarities. Supper over, I did what the general visitor to Kirtland usually does — climbed the long stairs leading to the outlook from the steeple of the Mormon temple, and viewed the country around. Directly in front to the east lay the valley, reaching toward Painesville and Grand River. The stream through the valley, which I fancied was a branch from the Chagrin, curious to explore a new route to the lake, had diverged, leaving its mother's arms and tickling itself as it ran like a wayward child through this charming valley to join its neighbor, the Grand. It wound itself idly and peacefully past the foot of Little Mountain, which lay a little to the south. The sun, dropping lower, leaves a lingering shadow upon the hilly boundary of the valley at the north, outlining finely the topography of the country. The sound of letting down of bars and the calling of "Co, boss; co, boss," was distinctly heard, and boys bringing cows to the barnyard to be milked reminded me of when I drove cows to and from pasture for sixpence a week. Off to the left was the roadway through the trees where Bob and I had come a couple of hours before. It looked beautiful now from the temple's spire. Farther to the left were indications of Willoughby and the sun dropping into the lake, leaving a background of glory in the sky. Looking to the right

P. S. Ryder, Photographer, Syracuse, N. Y.

EDNA MAY, THE SALVATION LASSIE.

toward Chester was a straight road gradually rising as far as could be seen. Leaving the fine outlook I came down to the ground and crossed over to the tavern. The whittlers were just "knocking off" for the day. The one who helped to lift my trunk out of the wagon commenced brushing the whittlings out from the wrinkles of his pants, then pushed the blade of his jack-knife shut to the first joint by pressing the back of the blade into the palm of his left hand, then to finish for a complete shutting, pressed the back of the blade against the calf of his leg, when it snapped deep into the handle with a sudden concussion, and he then said to his companion, "Lige, there's the best stuff in that blade of any I ever owned. It'll cut a hair slick as a razor. I traded for it with a fellow up in Chester and got the best end of the bargain by a good ways." Continuing, he said, "Well, Lige, I guess the wimmin folks must have supper ready by this time and mebby we'd better run home." "On second thought," said Ira, his companion, "let's take a 'thimbleful' of 'Bump's best' just for our appetites. Been somewhat off my feed lately." The "thimbleful" having been absorbed, he of the failing appetite wiped his mouth with the inside of his hand, pushing it over toward the Mormon temple, then dexterously turned his hand and with a return wipe brought that flexible feature back to the tavern side, got his lips adjusted together and with a loud smack, something between a smothered shudder and a strangle, he said, "Gosh, Lige, that's a stinger! I tell you, Gus Bump knows how to keep good whisky." "Yes," quoth Mr. Bump, "I got that whisky to wash my horse's legs with; of course it's good." "Well! just put it on the slate, Gus. I expect money from Jones soon, then I'll square up." "Good night, Gus. We'll be over tomorrow, some time." And the friends took a cut across lots in a direction south of the temple. "Yes," said Mr. Bump, partly as though communing with himself and partly observing to me, "I've heard that Jones story for a good while and am getting tired of it." "Prominent citizens?" queried I to Mr. Bump; "not Mormons?" "They're both good fellows in a way — not quite to the front as to energy, but good-natured, harmless citizens. They'd rather swap horses and dicker in pigs than chop cordwood." Then Bump's confidence, beginning to flow again, said, "There's Ira; had a good farm left him at his father's death three years ago. He sold off a strip of ten acres before he had put up a gravestone for the old man. Then he mortgaged what was left to buy a patent right upon a churn which didn't pan

E. G. Fountain, Photographer, Cleveland, O.

A MOMENT'S REST.

out well, or which he didn't properly push. The interest got behind and he put another mortgage on to clear that." " Not very good business management," I observed. " Well, no," said Mr. Bump. " They've gone into the chicken industry now. It don't tire them to have their hens lay eggs. They have some beautiful fowls though — Shanghais. The boss rooster can stand on the ground and eat corn off the head of an up-ended barrel."

Pushing his finger down into his pipe bowl, he continued, " They are talking some about going into the honey business. There's been a man around with a new-fangled hive, all partitioned off inside into compartments. They say the bees are so pleased with it that they work overtime. Why, if some fellow should come around selling wells already dug, Ira and Lige would be his first customers." As Mr. Bump seemed in a communicative mood, I thought I might properly ask some questions about the temple and the people who had worshiped in it. So I said, " I notice, Mr. Bump, that the doors of the temple are open, and all persons seem privileged to enter. Does any one have charge or control of it? " " No," said Mr. Bump, " it is as free as the common surrounding it. No one pretends to exercise any right or inclination to manage it. The people of the village and strangers who visit it go and come without question. It is free to all." " Do you think there would be any objection made by any one to my using one of the windows for the purpose of taking daguerreotype likenesses? " " Not the least," replied Mr. Bump. " If you think it would serve your purpose and you would like to go in and occupy it, do so freely. If you like, I will have your trunk sent over in the morning." I thanked him and said I would look the place over with reference to taking possession. " Are there any Mormons living here still? " I asked.

" Oh, yes," he replied, " it was a good deal for people to pull up, to leave home and friends; they couldn't take farms and property with them. The more earnest went; many are still here. They gave up holding services, and the temple has been abandoned as a place of worship for years." " Did you know the leaders, or any of them? " I asked. " Oh, yes. I knew Joseph Smith very well. We used to call him, in speaking of him, Joe Smith, as easy as people call me Gus Bump. He was a kindly man, and popular. He used to live down on the flats and had a house aside from his residence, where he secluded himself at times. and no one ventured to disturb him. While you are here, you will probably visit it.

A. J. Swanson, Photographer, Faribault, Minn.

FLEECY FRIENDS.

You will be interested in seeing it. I knew Sidney Rigdon, too.
He was rather reserved. Not so openly cheerful as ' Joe,' but a
good man.'' After some more chat of an indifferent nature, I bade
Mr. Bump good-night and retired.

Next morning I visited the temple and explored it with much
interest and curiosity. On entering upon the main floor, that which
would be in usual churches the auditorium, from the entrance
doors of which — there was one on each side — were aisles running
back to the altar. On either side of the aisles were broad pews,
separated into compartments by partitions of canvas, heavily painted
with white upon both sides. These partitions or curtains were
heavy as sails to a ship. They were fastened at bottom to large
rollers and rigged with ropes and pulleys at top like curtains in
theaters, for raising and lowering. Each curtain, with its heavy
roller, dropped into the space immediately behind the pew backs
and well in front of sitters in the pews, so they could be entirely
secluded from occupants of other pews — separated as completely
as though stowed in pigeon-holes. Or, if desired, the partition

curtains could be raised and the congregation seen as a whole.
Why these partitions, or for what purpose, was one of the things
I could never learn. There were a good many Mormons left
in Kirtland, but none who would talk of the rites or ceremonies
practiced in the temple. The room above was similar in size as
to floor space, but lower in height of ceiling. There were no
dividing partitions in this room. It was filled with pews, and
at either end with curious pulpits; as many as six pulpits. This
I fancied had been a section or department for the lesser saints, or
possibly for Sunday-school. In this room, which had broad and
high north windows, I determined to locate my studio. I built a
floor over the tops of the pew-backs, using them as joists; constructed a flight of steps with hand-rail, by which to ascend and
descend from the floor proper. With my background, my side-
screen, a little table and *Voigtlander* set up upon my studio floor, I
was ready for business. Here permit me to claim the unique
distinction of being the only photographer extant who ever had a
Mormon temple for a studio — a distinction of which I am proud.
On the evening of the day in which I took possession and fitted up
for business there was " company " at the Bump Hotel, and I was
invited to join the little party, which comprised a couple of former
instructors of the Young Ladies' Seminary, there on a visit, and a
number of their pupils who had met to do them honor. By way of
interesting the party I brought in a few daguerreotypes, which
were as good as letters of introduction, so eager were people in
those days to see likenesses. It happened that among those I
showed were pictures of a lady of prominence of Painesville, and
a handsome young man, also of Painesville, and who was well
known to the young lady pupils, and they were much pleased at
the chance meeting. I announced to the ladies that I had taken
possession of the temple for a studio and invited them to call. The
following morning, in good season, they came. After a little visiting, I invited them to sit in group, which invitation was pleasantly
accepted, and in a half hour thereafter I had the group, with other
likenesses, framed and hanging at the entrance door of the temple.
with my card as daguerreotypist. I had many interested visitors
from the start, and soon began to have customers. The residents
had not before had an opportunity to have likenesses taken at home,
as I was the first " likeness man " to visit Kirtland. Visitors from a
distance sometimes sat to me as an event of interest to be added to
their visit to the temple, of which the daguerreotypes were souve-

A. A. Morgan, Photographer, Port Huron, Mich.

nirs, as having likenesses taken *in a Mormon temple* was some-thing to be remembered. One day I made a visit to the famous residence and study of the prophet, Rev. Joseph Smith, which had never been occupied after his departure from it. I examined it with interest as a house with a history known to but few. The striking peculiarity of this house was a hole through the upper floor and ceiling large enough for a man to pass through easily. It looked as though a crowbar and an axe had been used in making it, from the floor above. No effort had been made to cut it to any particular form, or to smooth the edges; broken lath and plaster covered with cobwebs were hanging in ragged disorder from it. This, I was told, was the prophet's private sanctum, where it was believed at night he received his revelations, and where none intruded upon him. Whether he believed divine messages came more clear-cut through that ragged hole I know not. There seemed a superstition about the matter, antagonistic to confidences or willingness to talk, on the part of those I thought could have enlightened me. I simply certify to what I saw, and. am unable to give further information. In late years, while visiting in Palmyra, New York, near the hills where the sacred writings, upon plates of gold — the Mormon bible — were exhumed, a friend, in showing me the places of interest about the town, took me into an old building which had once been a business block but had fallen into disuse. He took me upstairs, through hallways of dirt and disorder, and finally into a large room which contained a few broken chairs, gloomy walls, old tables, dirty newspapers covering the floor, cobwebs hanging from the ceiling so covered with dust as to look like wrapping twine as to size. My friend told me I was in the room where the Mormons held their first meetings after finding their bible. Since their abandonment of Palmyra the room had been shunned and quite deserted. Upon the floor I found an old sword. I became at once interested, and wished to possess it; in fact, would have been glad to buy it. My friend told me no one would know anything of an owner and

advised me to take it with me, which I did. I had a young friend
who was much interested in collecting arms and curios. To him I
gave it and afterward saw it in his cabinet labeled " A relic of
Mormonism."   The temple at Kirtland, as the first, will always be
an object of interest.   It has always been and is visited by many.
In the tower, upon every available surface of the outlook, are
carved the names of visitors ambitious to record themselves as
such.   After remaining several weeks at Kirtland, I left one fine
morning for Chagrin Falls.   Going up the Chester road, the route
to Chagrin, I watched the temple until it was no longer to be seen.
I could never and will never forget my experience of that pleasant
summer.   Nauvoo, Illinois, after Kirtland, was next chosen as the
" Land of the Prophet," and plurality of wives.   Salt Lake City
now holds the cup.

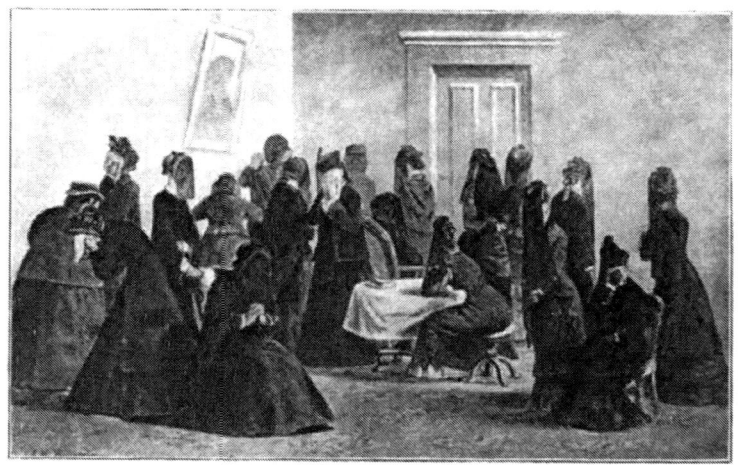

"OH, BRIGHAM!   HOW COULD YOU LEAVE US?"

When it came to pass that " Brigham," the saintly prophet,
was removed hence, Julia A. Moore, " The Sweet Singer of Michigan," took her pen in hand and composed the following touching
wail to his memory:

" 'Tis said that Brigham Young is dead,
   The man with nineteen wives:
The greatest Mormon of the West
   Is dead, no more to rise.
He left behind his nineteen wives
   Forsaken and forlorn;
The papers state his death was caused
   By eating too much green corn.

" It made him sick and very bad,
   Cholera morbus set in;
Doctors was brought from far and near,
   But none of them could help him.
Of course, he had the best of care —
   A wife for every call,
Nurses plenty, he had, you see,
   But he died and left them all.

'' Oh! death, it came, he had to go,
  And leave his weeping wives
To mourn the loss of one dear friend,
  The partner of their lives.
They stood around his dying bed,
  To see his life depart,
But few of them, do I believe,
  Wept with a broken heart.

'' Some, perhaps, did weep for grief,
  And some, perhaps, in woe;
And some, perhaps, were glad to see
  The old Mormonite go.
It left them free once more to roam,
  A husband to choose once more;
But some of them will never choose
  To live the same life o'er.

'' And as they stood around his bed
  Their hearts was filled with pain
To see him writhe in agony
  And hear him not complain.
It made them feel so very bad,
  They wept and mourned that morn,
And yet to think his death was caused
  By eating too much green corn.

'' At last his spirit fled away,
  And Brigham was no more:
Such weeping, wailing in a home
  Was never heard before.
And when his children came to see
  And look at him once more,
Their thoughts were often thus expressed:
  ' Our papa is no more.'

'' Brigham Young had nineteen wives,
  And children by the score;
Such a family for one man to own
  Was never known before.
His children is now left by him
  Forsaken and forlorn,
'Tis said they're often heard to say:
  ' Pa did eat too much green corn.'

'' Brigham's wives are in deep grief —
  It won't last very long,
Although 'tis sad their husband died
  By eating too much green corn.
He made a glutton of himself,
  Not thinking what he'd done,
Which caused the death of a Mormonite
  And the end of Brigham Young.''

Mrs. L. W. Bailey, Photographer. Lakewood, Ohio.

DIGGING FOR GOLD.

CHAPTER VII.

CHAGRIN FALLS.

Dr. H. M. Albaugh, Photographer, Cleveland, O.
ON THE CHAGRIN RIVER, OHIO.

I found Chagrin Falls to be a cheery, sociable and charming village. Dr. D. W. Bliss, who will be remembered as surgeon to President Garfield through his long suffering from the assassin's bullet, invited me to come to the Falls and start my business. He introduced me among his friends and kept a friendly eye on me. He asked me one day to drive over to Gates' Mills, a charming spot seven miles down the river, to visit his neighbor and chum, Dr. Tom Moore, an Irishman proud of his country and proud of his name — genial, kindly and tender of heart; voice soft, and brogue most delicious. It was a joy to see " the two o' them " together — a happiness to me to make the third. " Here's a health to thee, Tom Moore." Gates' Mills helped to make Chagrin more delightful, and visits were frequent. At the Falls I lived at Bayard's Hotel, a pleasant village inn, a stage house station on the Cleveland and Pittsburg pike. The mail was carried upon the coaches of this line and their arrival each day was an event. The Bayard House brightened up at the sound of the welcome horn before the coach

Louis Fleckenstein, Photographer, Faribault, Minn.

READY FOR THE WEDDING FEAST.

drove in sight. Old General Knox brought his chair out upon
the porch of the hotel, followed by guests or frequenters of the
house to witness the arrival of coach and passengers. The Bayard
boys hustled out their cart to receive and rush the mail bag across
the bridge to the postoffice, where Mr. Shaw, the village postmaster, stood in the door to receive it. Henry Breeze, a typical
joker and the admiration of the town, drove one of these coaches.
As he came winding down the hill, his horn, awakening echoes up
and down the valley and resounding from the hilltops, made a
pleasant sound. In his line, Henry was an artist. When he came
in sight at the turn of the road, he and his splendid four were a
picture; fine tassels of white hanging from every headstall, big
white rings of bone — in places doubled — trim the harness and
hold the reins which pass through them. A cowboy air as to hat,
rather broad in brim and turned straight up in front, proclaimed
championship for Henry as driver. As he came swinging down
the road to the passenger porch of the Bayard Hotel, it seemed the
easiest thing in life to come straight alongside and stop, but that

would be too easy for Henry; he would swing his long whip in a circle above his head, his leaders would take a sweep describing a circle to the outer opposite side of the street, with a run back across to the porch, coming to a sudden stop, the body of the coach rocking and pitching like a punt in a choppy sea, the off leader in the meantime going up on his hind feet and pawing the air with his fore, Henry pretending not to notice the trick he had taught his pet to do. Other drivers there were, safe, faithful and sure, who drove on the line and stopped in their turns at the house. But for showy, dare-devil air and smooth finish Henry was head and shoulders above all.

The Chagrin River (Indian for angry) went rushing and tumbling through the village. It seemed a capricious stream, indulging in fierce plunges, merry jumps, sudden whirls, dashing leaps, gentle ripples and calm, well-behaved placidity — all within a mile, and incidentally turning wheels which furnished power for axe factory, machine shops, paper mill and woolen factory, thus contributing to the industry of the village and lending a hand to enterprise, for which the little town was noted. It helped to make fortunes for a number of men. I was very fond of the river. I loved to saunter along its banks and enjoy the moods it induced, so much of variety and the picturesque did it present. I loved the liquid talk it made as it clambered over the stones which lay in its way — the gurgle and chatter seemed to me like a musical conversation between water and stones. As we sometimes find forms, faces and figures in a burning grate, and grotesque images and animals in the western sky, so I found voices in the water. When at leisure, or when studio hours were over, I walked down to the rapids to listen to what the water had to say. Like the sea which presents new phases each day, so I found the water to tell a new story or sing a new ditty. Farther down, the stream took on a more rugged phase, wilder, yet not less interesting in beauty. And here was the sculptured rock. At this point the water is deeper and more silent. The trees reaching their branches down farther and their bodies leaning over the bank toward the opposite side, where straight up from the water rises a smooth, flat-faced rock like a wall. It was discovered by some one that the face of this rock bore carvings — representations of birds, animals, and, most wonderful of all, Mother Eve is shown reclining, and, as though guarding her, is the serpent. By whom this work was done, or when, was a mystery. The general belief was that it was the work of Indians before white

VILLAGE FALLS, CHAGRIN RIVER, OHIO.

men inhabited the wilds of Ohio. A legend handed down "straight as a string" from father to son, of the tribe of the Cuyahogas, was to the effect that a young "brave," son of the chief, had wandered from the camp of his tribe upon the banks of the Cuyahoga River to the cascades of the Chagrin, upon whose banks he found an Indian maiden to whom he gave his heart. The brave thought her beautiful. Tradition has it that the babble of the rapids was taken up as an echo of the love-making between the Indian lovers, and the delighted water, then started, has kept it up ever since in memory of the wooing. The sculptured rock is alleged to be a valentine carved by the brave — an outpour of his heart to the maiden. Tradition further says that upon a fine October day "at high noon" was solemnized the nuptials of J. Marmaduke Sunshine and Lilian Maud Wade-in-the-Water, the ceremony being performed by the chief of the Cuyahogas. The bride wore "frills and feathers." The groom was clad in doeskin, garnished with scalps. The decoration was the glorious foliage of the forest, painted by October suns and harvest moons. The happy couple went by canoe on a three weeks' trip to their cousins, the Maumees, and were "at home to their friends" on their return. I am indebted for this legend to a talented member of the "Artemus Ward Club" of newspaper reporters, who claimed to have it from "an honest Indian," a true descendant of the distinguished parents. I confessed to the reporter that it seemed a pretty story and was no doubt true. "True," retorted the man of pad and pencil, "that Indian has the arrow-heads to prove it. If you doubt it in the least you can take the first trolley to Chagrin and interview the talking rapids, and there stands the rock with the zoölogy still upon it." "Well," said I, "where did you find the Indian, and what is his name?'' ''His name is Ti-ock-ne-o-ga Joe, and he is one of Buffalo Bill's stage robbers. I saw him last summer.''

The young people of the village took me in as a worthy addition to their circle. Of the young ladies I met, I soon found one to be '' the dearest girl in the world.'' To a young man early in his twenties this is not an unusual happening, so I justified myself in finding Chagrin Falls to have and to hold every charm of which a dear, bright village could be possessed. A certain cottage seemed to be the heart of the town and shed a pleasant glow upon all within reach. The porch, the hospitable seats thereon, the entrance gate swinging in toward the cottage, suggesting welcome, all contributed to voluntary enslavement of a willing heart. In her presence I was in a halo of happiness. A sweet modesty mixed with

SCULPTURED ROCK, CHAGRIN FALLS, OHIO.

harmless witchery of mischief and innocence was the nature of that sunny girl. It was not strange that under such fascinations a susceptible and rather timid young fellow should have lost his balance — not at all strange. We were excellent friends. We sometimes wandered down to the talking rapids, I hoping the glib water would help me to say or her to understand what I would like to be said, but we returned without the '' ice being broken.'' There is something — an unseen and unexplainable something — which cautions a man against venturing too far. I found out one day what was the matter. It was another fellow, who had a stronger claim.

John Rösch, Photographer, White Plains, N. Y.

NICK AND I.

One day I boarded the stage behind Henry Breeze's prancers for a trip to Cleveland, the city I had carried in my mind for two years. I made straight for Mr. Johnson's gallery of daguerreotype portraits. I was met by a young man who struck me as an upstart — quite destitute of good manners. I thought his style of meeting a stranger, whether visitor or customer, was faulty. In a manner too abrupt to be courteous he asked, " Do you want anything? " I replied that I wished to see Mr. Johnson and to examine the specimen pictures. In reply he said, " Johnson is not in," and abruptly left the room. I took a reasonable time to examine the work. While I found it good, it was not quite up to my expectations, and I was a bit disappointed. I had seen a good deal and had progressed somewhat since the day I bought the formula for making " dry quick." Mr. Johnson did not return. I went out and took the return stage to Chagrin Falls without seeing the man I desired so much to meet, but had learned a lesson worth the price of the trip.

CHAPTER VIII.

BEDFORD, OHIO.

Tinker's Creek is wild and savage enough to seem out of place in a peaceful little village only a dozen miles from Cleveland. It runs through a gorge of rock a hundred feet deep, the walls of which are nearly perpendicular. The bed of the stream is clogged with heavy, broken rocks; washed and smoothed by the action of the water through the centuries, which in winter are covered with masses of ice — cruelly cold. From the seams of the rocky banks, bushes and small trees of rugged growth are thrust out, and in the glen are nooks never reached by the sun, where on hot days visitors may sit in the grateful shade and listen to the monotonous murmur of the running water. Upon the top of the west bank sat Bedford town, with its two hotels, its public square, its complement of stores and shops, its snug homes and its friendly people. It was a trading center for a farming district of half a dozen miles around.

At this time the Cleveland & Pittsburg Railroad was under construction through Bedford, which gave the town an unusual activity, and spanning the chasm of Tinker's Creek was being built a trestle bridge or scaffolding upon which to carry the stringer for the truss. This manner of work was a novelty to the people of the village, as it rose from the broken rocks in the bed of the creek, a succession of timbers end upon end to grade level, where the rails were to be laid. A goodly number of people were in daily attendance until the stringers were stretched from shore to shore. A venturesome lot of people possessed of a whim to be the first to cross started upon the foolhardy feat — a number of women as well as men joined in the venture — the craze struck me, too, and I started. As I approached the center, the point highest from the rocky bottom, where to look down was suggestive of a fall to sure death, I realized what a poor exhibition of bravery it was. If I could have turned back I would gladly have done so, but the fool procession was behind as well as in front, and there was no help for it; I had to move with the crowd. I would have been thankful for a hand-rail; the inclination to get down and creep along upon the timbers with

George Lee, Photographer, Cleveland, O.

BEDFORD GORGE.

the advantage of being able to grasp them with my hands was upon me; but no one else did so, not even the ladies. There was not a little squeal or scream from them. There were no attempts at conversation; no comments or banterings; they were attending closely to the business in hand. A false step, a loss of balance, would have been quite out of order just then. At last we reached the opposite bank and thankfully stood upon solid ground.

I noticed the crowd was willing to walk a good half mile around rather than to recross the chasm upon a single timber. I got so many dollars from the contractor for daguerreotypes of the structure that I was enabled to " speak well of a bridge which had carried me safely over." A few years later a broader bridge of stone, with deep arches and double tracks, replaced the wooden one. In this autumn of my stop at Bedford was held a camp-meeting within two miles of the village. Never having attended a meeting of this kind I determined on the following Sunday to do so. One of the acquaintances I had made in Bedford joined me for companionship, and together we went. On entering the woods which led to the camp we found deep cut wagon tracks winding along, dodging the trees where wagons had not been before, but where they were on this day in great numbers. There were farm wagons and carriages from a distance of miles around, from surrounding villages, and even from Cleveland. Horses hitched to trees, horses unhitched from wagons and feeding from them. There were tents and hastily built shanties; there were temporary tables of boards upon which to spread food from baskets; there were even cooking-stoves, and pots boiling suspended from poles fastened to the trunks of trees. There were families of husbands, wives and children, and there were neighbors and neighborly people. There were young fellows and girls come for a lark, as though it were a township picnic. There were preachers of great power, and "a wonderful outpouring," it was said, had resulted from the preaching through the week, and this day, Sunday, a great manifestation of the Spirit was expected. For the preacher's stand a large platform had been built, and hastily constructed seats prepared. On the outskirts of this auditorium, among the wagons, tents and sheds, where the young and thoughtless were gathered, it appeared more like a gala day than an assemblage for divine worship. There had been a heavy shower in the early morning. As the time for opening services was drawing near it was discovered that the front rows of seats — those known as "anxious seats," being nearest the preaching platform, were on low ground, and water was standing there.

The Rev. Shouter, in charge of the meetings, was a stirring man, a gifted preacher and a good organizer; he was quick to see the objection to the water in that particular spot and quietly ordered some straw to cover it. Some was brought, such as could be spared, from tents and wagons, but it was quite insufficient. Then, like one born to command, he stepped upon the platform and called out, "Here you brothers; wherefore stand ye idle? The ground is wet in front of the pulpit. We want straw, we want more straw — souls may be lost for the want of straw! Go to brother Skinner's barn and get straw; this wet must be sopped up." As the time approached for speaking to commence, the seats began to be filled, and it was noticeable that the audience was made up of earnest faces, and that the ladies of the congregation did not affect elaborate or gorgeous toilets. Going to meeting in the woods did not require silk gowns. These women had come to hear expounded the word of God in the hope of divine grace being given them. The solemnity of the woods, "the gathering in the wilderness," as it were, the whisperings of the Great Spirit through the stilled breath of the air, the boundless dome of heaven above, all contributed to serious, sincere solemnity. The feeling of getting nearer to God here than

BEDFORD GLENS, BEDFORD, OHIO.

under roofed churches fills the mind and satisfies the listener. The word comes unobstructed by groined arches or architectural fashionings. Nature gives approval and benediction to God's children who gather together in His name to seek His blessings. This was noticeable in the faces of the congregation here assembled. The Rev. Shouter arose from the rude bench provided for himself and his assistants, stepped to the front of the platform and gave out the hymn,

" Come, ye sinners, poor and needy,
Weak and wounded, sick and sore,"

with the request that all voices be heard. The singing was taken up with a heartiness and vigor that made the woods resound. Prayer followed, and then came the preaching. I cannot recall the text of the good man, but his sermon was earnest and powerful; his appeals in behalf of sinners, and especially those for whom he was pleading, were searching and magnetic. Many were visibly affected. When the sermon was closed he announced that after the next singing a season of prayer would follow, and a request was made that the mourners of the day before who had not received the full blessing should take seats on the front row. I could but notice there seemed much of a business air attending the preparation. Those especially gifted and powerful in prayer were arranged upon the platform, and were called upon by Rev. Shouter to lead and to follow, according to their force and ability as pleaders for anxious souls. I noticed among the mourners a colored woman who seemed strangely affected. The man who accompanied me from our hotel and who sat beside me, said, " Keep your eye upon her, she is a subject for ' the power.' " My inexperience inclined me to ask what he meant by " the power." He replied that it was a condition of

extreme excitement — a religious frenzy — "the operation of the
Spirit" — to which colored people were more sensitive than whites,
and they "give way" to it more readily.   Continuing, he said, "I'm
from Virginia, and have seen on the plantations much of their ' re-
joice ' and hallelujah and listened to their hallelujah voices, which are
really in a way impressive.   They shout and jump, sometimes fall
down and go into a trance condition, in which they remain for a
longer or shorter period.   They call it ' coming through,' a process
of being converted from sin to righteousness.   They fall down in
sin and awaken purified, usually singing, crying and rejoicing."   I
was keeping an eye upon the colored woman, who seemed under
extreme excitement.   She threw her arms up, she shouted and
cried, begging for God's mercy.   Suddenly backward she went
over one of the seats, kicking and floundering.   A rush was made
for her by those nearest.   After a little she quieted down — had
evidently gone into the trance which my informant had told me
about.   Her fall, however, seemed to provoke unsuppressable
laughter, and broke up the meeting.   There was no going farther
with that session.   I thought the general merriment seemed sacrilegious, and in my mind resented it.   I heard one woman ask
another what the people were laughing about.   The reply was,
through suppressed laughter, " Well, the situation was laughable
and ridiculous — that colored woman was not properly clad for such
a mishap.   Poor thing, I was very sorry for her; but it was so
funny."   And the woman laughed again in spite of herself.   That
portion of the dismissed congregation that returned to Bedford
village did not maintain unbrokenly the serenity of the Sabbath
usually observed in returning from morning services.   Surely from
the sublime to the ridiculous is but a step.   My room in Gray's
Hotel was in the back part, overlooking the kitchen yard, where
the crowing and cackle of chickens and the odor of frying ham were
accompaniments to the rattle of dishes.   The morning after the
camp-meeting episode I heard issuing from the kitchen a contralto
voice, soft and deep, half humming, half singing hymns which I
recalled as having been sung at the meeting in the woods.   With
increasing earnestness, with a thrill of rhythm and refrain, the
voice poured out in unrestrained abandon the " Waker," " Come,
ye sinners, poor and needy."   I gave way to my curiosity — went
into the breakfast room; took a look into the kitchen, and there
was the colored woman of yesterday, sure enough.   She was our
new cook, wonderfully skilled in fried chicken and corn dodgers.

CHAPTER IX.

MUDDY ROADS.

In looking back upon the callow days of my wanderings I am impressed with the good fortune I found at every step. People attached a more grave importance to having likenesses taken then. It was more the parents having likenesses taken for the children, a matter more seriously considered; something more in the way of duty, possibly a last duty — certainly a sacred one — from parents to children, a legacy of love.

I had settled upon Medina, a place twenty miles distant from Bedford, for my winter quarters. It was the middle of November and the roads were getting bad. I employed a man with a strong team and as light a wagon as would do, in anticipation of mud. We started, leaving Bedford and Tinker's Creek behind. As we got beyond the village limits, inside of which greater care had been taken to keep ruts and holes filled and packed, we found mud enough to sling at political candidates throughout

R. W. Seaman, Photographer, Kansas City, Mo.

THE CITY STAR.

the States, and for children to supply the pie market for Ohio indefi-
nitely.   A lake of liquid mud, with small islands cropping up here
and there, covered the entire width of the road, and between the
road-bed and the fences deep-cut tracks of wagons were seen.   It
was a discouraging outlook, much worse than we had expected, but
having started we resolved to go through.   It was a hard pull for
our horses.   Our wagon wheels were pulling up chunks of mud at
every revolution, which fell back with a splash into the thinner
surface and sank out of sight.   Occasionally we met an adventurous
navigator plodding his way with a scowl upon his face, sullen and
silent, his wagon, horses and harness bespattered.   To speak of
mud would not be taken for a joke — perhaps we had better not ask
how far we were from Medina.   There are times when men do not
want to talk.   The man at my side did not encourage conversation.
I did not feel quite cheerful myself.   It was muddy; we could
neither of us change the situation, and so fell into a communion of
silence.   The few vehicles we met were not out for pleasure; they
were " paddling their own canoes " the same as we were ours; to
keep well in the channel, avoiding snags and hidden rocks was
good fortune.   We wallowed and lurched all day, at dusk entered
the port of Medina and dropped anchor for the night.   Here at the
hotel we met Mr. Joseph Whitmore, daguerreotypist and postmaster
of the village.   I told him my purpose had been to stop through the
winter.   He assured me that Medina could not support two daguerreotypists, and recommended Elyria, thirty miles distant, a larger
and brighter town, and no daguerreotype man.   We took an early
start for Elyria.   It was a long and tedious drive, the roads still
muddy, but not so bad as the day before.   At Richfield we stopped
for dinner and rest for ourselves and team.   There I found a
likeness man named Scripture.   I was more impressed with his
name than with the quality of his work.   We took up our drive
again after dinner and by patient and continuous plodding arrived
at Elyria just at dark.   My heavy trunk unloaded and our team
stabled, we sat down to our supper at the Beebe House, a pair of
tired men.   It began to rain as we arrived and was a dreary evening.   The Cleveland & Toledo Railway, now a section of the Lake
Shore & Michigan Southern, was being surveyed through Elyria,
and a gang of surveyors came in, wet and weary from their day's
tramp.   Their high boots were splashed to the knees with mud,
and so were their surveying instruments, rods, poles and chains.
The hungry men ordered supper, and while it was being prepared

Louis F. Jansen, Photographer, Buffalo, N. Y.

HOW DO YOU LIKE IT?

they sat around the big stove to warm and dry themselves. The steam from their wet clothing began to rise, lading the air with a suggestion of wet boots and rubber coats. One of the party, a boy in his teens and delicate in appearance, fell asleep in the grateful warmth. A few people belonging to the house and an occasional dropper-in exchanged greeting with the surveyors, commented upon the disagreeable evening, inquired about the progress of the work and how the road was getting along. Supper was announced and they went into the dining-room like men with appetites. I began to study those whom I felt must be citizens and possibly future acquaintances. I was commencing a mental impression taking. I usually find impressions without prejudice a pretty reliable guide. We can like or dislike people at sight; can in some way make acquaintance without speaking. I went to the windows and looked out upon the street to get impressions there. The lamps upon the corners, in store and shop windows; the colored lights of a drug store, all looked blinky and sickly through the wet glass. I was forced to admit that the place did not present a cheerful appearance. I concluded to go to my room to write a letter to my mother, and go to bed. I certainly was tired enough to go to sleep. I was nearer being homesick than any time since leaving the parental roof. The Beebe House was quite a smart hotel for a village of three thousand population, and was a source of pride to the proprietor whose name it bore. Adjoining it was a business block continuation, occupied as stores, bank, postoffice, telegraph office on the ground floor, and the floors above as business offices, legal, medical and otherwise. Upon this floor I secured rooms for my studio. In front of the hotel was a pleasant park surrounded by residences and public buildings. Opposite the park on the main street was the commercial block, which was occupied as stores and for business purposes. Elyria being the county seat or capital of Lorain county, was a stirring trade center, as was evidenced by crowds of teams in the street and the busy stores, especially on Saturdays, which, more than any other day of the week, was market and shopping day for the farmers and their families. " Baldwin's " and " Mussey's " stores were busy places. Wagon-loads of grain and farm products to sell, household goods and groceries to purchase, made stirring times. The Germans, of whom there were many, made themselves quite at home and as comfortable as possible in the back part of these stores. There they ate their lunches as composedly as though they were in their own kitchens. I saw

Knaffl Bros., Photographers, Knoxville, Tenn.

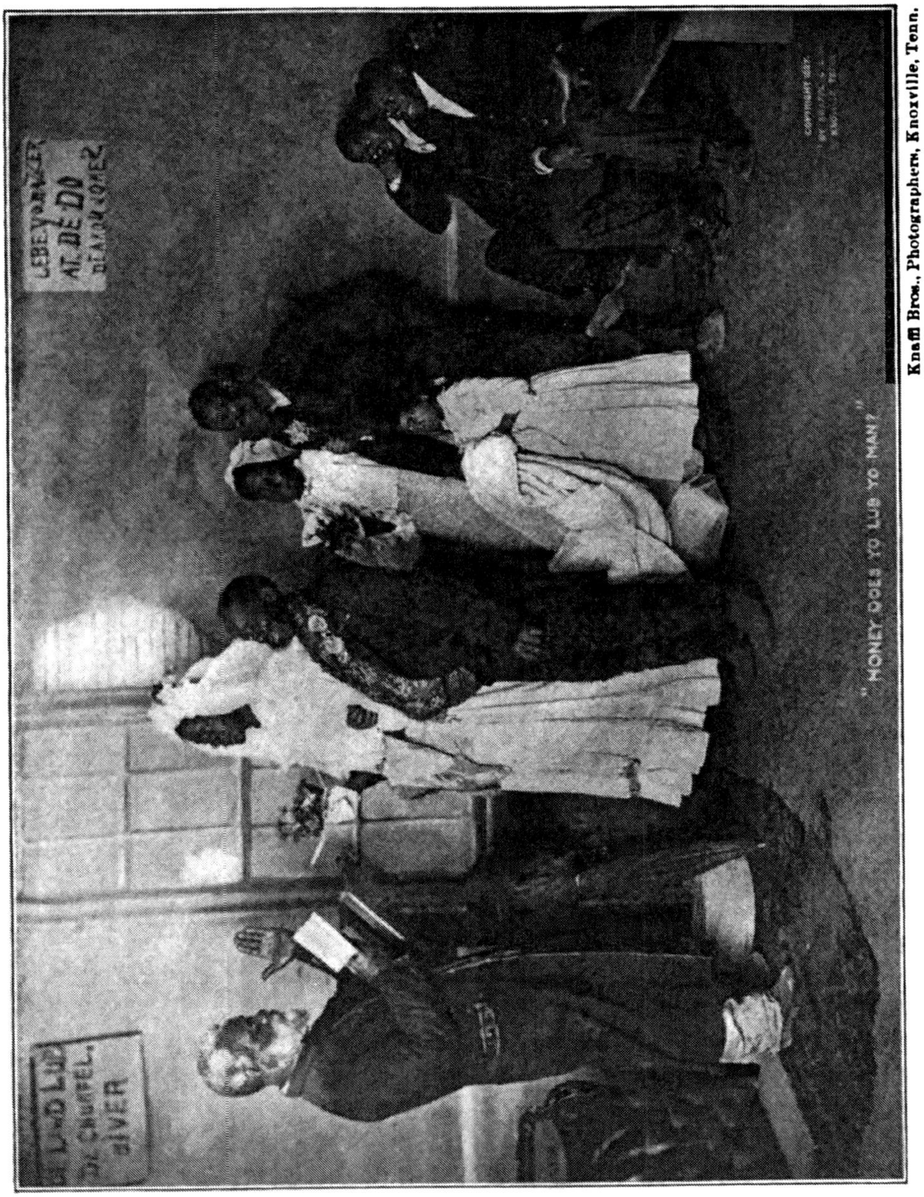

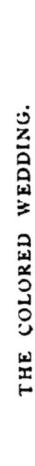

THE COLORED WEDDING.

one day a kindly-faced and friendly-looking old German woman reach down and pull a clay pipe from behind her garter and commence her smoke as matter-of-fact and as unhesitatingly as she ate her bread. She gave a picture of enjoyment pure and simple. Elyria is an island held in the arms of the east and west branches of the Black river, which empties into Lake Erie at Lorain. These two arms of the river form a junction a half mile from the park and main business street. To assert their charms in a picturesque display, each wears a bracelet at the wrist in a dashing cascade before clasping hands at the junction. The beauty of these streams, the surrounding rocks, the rapids, the overhanging trees upon either shore and the rugged banks, are allegorically laid at the feet of this picturesque child of Ohio, whose charms are famous. Artists from many studios visit here to sing praises to her beauty in sketches by brush and pencil. The richest and daintiest offering to the artist is here spread out for his pleasure. My fondness for the beautiful in nature found here much to feed upon. At evening before twilight I found my reserved front seat, which no one else disputed, and enjoyed it to my heart's content.

On moonlight nights, after " Wils " Ryan, the miller, had shut up shop and gone home, I would lounge on the grass beside the old mill with its great, drippy water-wheel, and enjoy the pleasing rhythm of the falling water, splashing and dripping continuously and soothingly, inducing me to indulgence in waking dreams which led me pleasantly to Ithaca and the old Cascadilla, whose dashing water I so dearly loved.

A young man to whom I was drawn because of his " happy-go-lucky " nature, and who was so filled with sunshine that it seemed to radiate upon all who came about him, wanted to learn to make daguerreotypes, and I took him for a pupil. His name was Charles Park. He became a faithful student, and ultimately took a prominent place in the ranks of photography as a skilful and successful practitioner. We were congenial and as progressive as our opportunities permitted. As we were going in the same direction, we pulled well together. My three years' advance in the work gave me an acknowledged lead which he recognized and to which he deferred. When he became sufficiently skilled to work independently of me, I sometimes sent him out to the smaller towns, that he might acquire a settled confidence in his ability. On his return from one of these outings, of the money he brought in was a silver dollar he had received for a likeness. The coin had a history.

The man who paid it to him was father to a family of eleven children, every one of whom had cut its teeth upon that coin.   Park
said that the mother was very loath to part with it, and made him
promise to hold it for a time, subject to exchange for another dollar
which she would bring in.   Sure enough, she came the following
week, a distance of ten miles, to redeem it, and was delighted that
it had been saved for her.   There was to be a school exhibition on
the coming Saturday night at this little village, so the proud mother
told us, and her eldest daughter, the first biter of the coin, was to
take part in a play.   So earnest was the mother's invitation for us
to come over that we agreed to go.

A. H. Mowry, Photographer, Ashland, O.

OLD FOLKS AT HOME.

CHAPTER X.

AMATEUR THEATRICALS.

Private theatricals are interesting as a departure from robust professional dramatic work, a freshness and originality cropping out at unexpected times and places to challenge and amuse an audience. Doubtless all people of both sexes have a secret desire to " tread the boards " and astonish friends with latent and unsuspected talent which has lurked in their breast and been smothered for opportunity to come forth and shine. The world knows not what may have been lost in unrevealed genius or what it has escaped by its suppression. The enjoyment found in some plays by amateurs quite overbalances the pleasure found in serious professional performances. We thought the present opportunity was one not to be missed, and drove over to the village in the afternoon, and put up at the tavern in whose ballroom the play was to be given. We were well received by the landlord, given a good supper, and I secured a room for the night, as after the play it would be too late to return. The leading man, or the hero of the tragedy of the evening, was pointed out to us as the brightest scholar in the school and particularly strong in declamation. Not exactly with ostentation, but with a tread of consciousness, he walked up and down the office of the hotel as though studying his part or anticipating a triumph. He was not in the least embarrassed because people were regarding him with attention — he was to be the hero of the play and was not ashamed to be known as such. As evening came on an unusual activity was apparent — people were coming in, passing through the hallway and upstairs. The landlord came to us with a suggestion that if we wished to secure good seats perhaps we had better go up. Of course we desired good seats, and we went up, none too soon, for the room was being rapidly filled. There was a good bit of interest in noting the audience, the expectant and impatient manner of it. The room was lighted by lamps hung upon the walls, with tin reflectors behind to throw added strength of light, which was not, however, a great success. There were no footlights, no chandeliers for a more brilliant lighting;

S. L. Cassar, Photographer, Valetta, Malta.

ENTRANCE TO HARBOR, VALETTA, MALTA.

no orchestral overture to help kill time before curtain rising; no
" cat calls " from the boys; no impatient stamping of feet — just a
patient wait.   The drop curtain was of plain white cloth, and thin,
so the actors and actresses showed plainly through.   The stage
being lighted more than the auditorium proper, the company was
more in sight than the audience, and without knowing it at all.
The stage was green-room without being aware of its publicity.
The posings and primpings of the players were a free show, and, I
fancied, a better one through the curtain than we would see when
it was raised.   A little girl sitting beside me who had a vial of pep-
permint essence to which she would touch her tongue occasionally,
I found open to conversation, which was carried on between us in
a low tone.   She gave me important information as to who the
actors were that would appear.   She pointed out her sister who was
upon the stage and who would take a part.   I was satisfied she was
one of the eleven whose teeth had come through upon the dollar,
and here was my little friend of the essence, whose gums had
yielded to the silver disk.   I was in luck to make such valuable

finds. At last the stage was cleared, the curtain raised, and a young lady came blushing upon the stage, and in a sweet voice pitched to a pleasant tune told us in song, "I love the merry, merry sunshine, it makes the heart so gay." She looked so innocently sweet I did not blame the sun for shining upon her. The song completed, she withdrew, loudly applauded.

The next number was a piece " spoken " by a young man. We did not quite make head or tail to it; the gist of it was, however, the revelation of some crookedness on the part of another young fellow, and the declaration of the relater that the other fellow of crooked tendency " Had better let the Gold Watch be." The reader will kindly pardon the obscure surroundings of this legend. It is given as clearly as we received it. Thinking that the elocutionist needed encouragement, Mr. Park and myself applauded right heartily, and were rewarded by a nice bow from the performer. These two numbers were merely a prelude to the tragedy which was the main attraction of the evening and was to come on here. I am again under embarrassment on account of my inability to give the name of the tragedy or even the names of the characters, as no program was on distribution nor announcement made. The curtain rose on three characters — two males and a female. The males seemed to be made up for villains with heavy eyebrows and false beards. They wore short shoulder cloaks which permitted the right arm entire freedom in case some sword business should be necessary; hats slouched; high boots with trousers tucked inside. By their sides hung sabers with basket handles and square, blunt ends, such as are used by pirates on deck of ships when attacked by men-of-war. The female was dressed in white with a blue ribbon around her waist. She was seated at a table with needlework in her hands; a few stitches were taken, but she was too agitated to continue. The males strode across the stage from side to side, with an " unhand-me-villain " air, glaring at each other as they met, their sabers clanking with an ugly sound. The one with the heaviest eyebrows opened the conversation by saying: " Villain, you have wronged me." This led to hard words from the other and was the beginning of a dispute in which very mean and provoking things were said on both sides. It was evident the difference was about the young lady and each seemed bent upon carrying his point. The young lady seemed much distressed to be the cause of the quarrel. Finally the most persistent of these seemingly bad men turned abruptly to the young lady and said, " Prythee, fair

J. W. Anderson, M. D.. Photographer, Washington, D. C.

AS SWEET BY ANY OTHER NAME.

Genevieve, choose between us." It was easy to see the appeal was most trying, as she arose from her chair, put her work carefully upon the table, clasped her hands and said convulsively, " Oh, De-haldimer, I can not, I can not."

Then Dehaldimer, evidently broken up at her reply, hissed between his teeth, " Zounds, fellow! Draw, and protect thy caitiff life!" and now commenced a fierce combat. Heavy blows were aimed at each other; lunges sharp and hard were driven. He who seemed the weaker was forced upon his knee, and the other, seeing his advantage, hammered hard blows upon the upturned saber as he walked around the disabled antagonist. The plucky fellow upon his knee weakened not at all, but kept up the fight to the admiration of the audience. By a quick turn of the wrist the man upon his knee flipped the saber out of the other's grasp and it went flying across the stage; then, dagger in hand, rushed upon his disarmed antagonist. To give realism of effect the man who had to be killed wore a bladder filled with something like blood under his shirt, and as the dagger came close, the victim considerately held the shirt open to facilitate the stabbing. The imitation blood gushed out, covering himself and a portion of the stage. He partly fell, and partly laid himself down to die, while the conqueror knelt beside him, raising his right hand and his eyes heavenward, while his left was pressed against his breast. At this juncture Genevieve let down her front hair, a generous strand on each side, as deliberately as though undressing for bed. She wound a strand around each hand and began to pull real hard, and let loose a series of wild screams as she knelt by the other side of the slain actor. The curtain went down slowly and solemnly, and the audience filed out deeply impressed — a man had been slain before their very eyes. During the night, from the bed occupied by Park, I heard what seemed a suppressed agitation. I feared he was ill, possibly coming under the paroxysm of a fit. I hurriedly went to him and asked what was the matter. By the pale moonlight coming through the window I saw him rise to a sitting posture, clasp his hands and exclaim, " Oh, Dehaldimer! I can not, I can not." More than half a century has passed. It has been my fortune to witness many of the world's greatest artists and their wonderful representations, but with them all in plain view, that evening with the amateurs holds firm grasp upon my memory, and is recalled with greater pleasure than any performance I can remember.

CHAPTER XI.

IN NATURAL COLORS.

C. W. Schlde, Photographer, Elyrla, O.

EAST BRANCH FALLS, ELYRIA, OHIO.

In the year 1850 was announced a great discovery in the daguerreotype process. No less a discovery than taking with the picture the natural colors of life. A clergyman by the name of L. L. Hill, of Westkill, a village on the Hudson river, New York, was the fortunate discoverer. What Daguerre gave the world — an image in *light* and *shade* — was an astonishment, but it lacked the perfection in color of nature and life. Certainly a great lack and regret. Now came the reverend gentleman with *his* discovery to make the infant art complete. We might now expect to see the blue or violet eye in its perfection, and peach-tinted cheeks, rose-leaf lips, the varied shades of gold in baby's hair would delight us. Bright and rich colors of ribbon and dress of course were not overlooked in Mr. Hill's discovery. Everything was said to be there. The newspapers said these things — and it is as easy to make vivid and pleasing colors as weak or fady, at the editorial table. Daguerreotype men of prominence from the large cities visited Mr. Hill, and, it was alleged, made tempting offers for his secret of producing natural colors. He would not sell. He guarded it closely, all pictures were carefully sealed from examination or inspection. All customers were cautioned against permitting likeness men to remove the glass that covered the picture, or in any way to tamper with them. Things much coveted and not attainable are more wildly desired than the easy things of life. So the Hillotype was pined for by many. We fellows at a distance from New York had never seen one of the Hillotype pictures; for that matter, very few had. We were quite dependent upon newspaper accounts, and were inflamed by them. The business of likeness-taking was just about ruined; people were waiting for the pictures in natural colors. The sinful likeness man, with scant reverence for " the cloth," made hard criticisms upon " that minister," Hill, who had paralyzed the business, saying " he had better stick to his preaching and let picture-taking alone." It was said that Hill preached on the Sabbath, gave " talks " and prayer-meetings on Friday evenings, and during the week took in many a dollar for Hillotypes. The practice of men of the camera in those days to give a semblance of life coloring to the likeness before putting it in its case was to touch up with dry prepared color with a camel's-hair brush or pencil, such parts as cheeks, lips, etc., which required color, but the highly polished surface of the plate did not readily receive the pigment, and it could not forcibly be made to adhere. The Hillotype was anxiously awaited as a remedy to this imperfect method. Before the keen edge of anxiety was allowed to become dulled by much delay, the craft throughout the country received circulars announcing the publication of a book by the Rev. L. L. Hill, giving the history and practice of the daguerreotype; valuable formulas, and methods of work complete. The most startling feature of the coming work was that full and complete instructions were to be given for the production of the Hillotype. The price of the book was $5 by mail, postpaid. No book would be mailed until the entire edition was ordered, the money to accompany the order, of course. Those who ordered first would be first to receive the book, as all would be mailed in regular list order — first come, first served. Well, we all tumbled over each other at the doors of the postoffices to be first to post our money. In the interval of some weeks, in which I was waiting, I was busy making Hillotypes in my mind. I was studying diligently — nothing escaped me. I noticed carefully the color of eyes, of complexions, of rosy, well-rounded cheeks and ripe lips. Blonde and golden hair had a special fascination for me. I made mental sittings in Hillotype of all the fine subjects I saw. I made a list of subjects I should invite to pose for me when I received my

COMRADES.

book. I became so impressed with red hair in my study that I have never gotten over it. Little " tots " of children with golden hair were my special delight; men with red noses had an interest for me. I certainly dreamed out some beautiful work in those days. At last the book came. I entered my little studio, locked the door — that I might have all the joy to myself without interruption — went direct to the chapter on Hillotype, which was the last in the book. I read with bated breath. The book revealed to me that after the plate was finished, ready for casing, it should be flowed with a thin wash of transparent glue dissolved in distilled water. This, on drying over a spirit lamp, would give the surface of the plate a "tooth," a mild, sticky coating to which the color, applied as usual with a camel's-hair pencil, would adhere, as it would not to the highly polished surface of the plate. I could sympathize with the little girl who found her doll stuffed with sawdust. I realized that the reverend gentleman had given me as smooth a sell as I could have received from an accomplished horse-trader in a "swap." I do not remember announcing by advertisement, or otherwise, the Hillotype as one of my possessions. I do not recall an instance of any daguerreotype man making a claim to ownership of that wonderful improvement to our young art. I fancy they felt it was "one on them," and they did not care to parade the fact. If the reverend "discoverer" be still on earth he doubtless takes an occasional laugh up his sanctimonious sleeve on recalling the "easy scoop he took on the boys." He surely is entitled to credit for the habit of discovering natural colors in photographs; he being the first. Every few years we have new announcements of the alleged discovery of color photography which, as a matter of fact, is yet to be perfected. The new discoverer is usually a Parisian scientist, and the discovery is made after a patient research, or accidentally stumbled upon. It happens sometimes that a discoverer crops up at Oshkosh, or elsewhere. These discovery announcements are no doubt gratifying to the persons whose names are connected with them, but they are misleading and soon join the "great majority."

It is true that methods have been discovered and employed by means of which, from repeated printings of different plates, a means partly photographic and partly mechanical, color effect is given, and some subjects, like fruits or flowers, are made to appear very natural, but are not absolutely correct. Color may be given by reflection or transmission through colored media, the results of which in some cases are beautiful and a delight to the eye. These methods are ingenious, and while by their means a photograph may appear to be in natural colors, it is not. The foundation is a plain gray photograph, and dependent upon the reflection or transmission of colored glasses thrown upon or covering it to give color effect. Photographing in natural colors, or natural colors in photographs, is a misnomer — a method of imparting color to photographs would seem more correct. To remove the glass or glasses which give color is to reveal the plain gray photograph which forms the foun-

dation or body of the picture. A person is not red,
green or blue because seen
through glasses of these
colors. The desire to
attain wonderful results
stimulates efforts of dis-
c o v e r y and invention.
When the real can not be
compassed, a semblance
may be accepted. The
Indian, whose ambition
was to walk over the rain-
bow, had to be content
with walking under it.
Birds of the air navigate
space above the earth;
they rest at anchor in the
blue; they sail lazily about;
they take a sudden lurch
and dive; they tack; they
make into the wind; they
run before it; out to sea
they go, and are lost to
view. It appears quite
simple. The Creator of
all made it possible. The
ingenuity of man has not
yet devised or built a
machine to successfully
rival the bird, though
flying m a c h i n e s have
become as plentiful as
color methods in photog-

EASTER MORNING.

raphy. What I understand to be *natural colors* in photographs, the
actuality of which would be a blessing to photography and photographers, is that the colors *be born with and in the image* as it comes
into existence from the camera, or as it is evolved by the developer
from seeming nothingness to a reality. A straightforward, rather
than a complicated, round-about means involving various processes,
impractical for general use. An artificial pretense is not the real

thing. A negro is in natural color from birth. A white man blackened up for a cakewalk or a banjo solo is an imitation, a deception, and *not* in natural color.   Thankful and appreciative for what has been given in devices for imparting color to monochromatic camera products, and hopeful for the future, natural colors in photographs are, to my mind, I regret to say, *not yet*.   It was at Elyria that I received my book on how to make Hillotypes.   That was before the advent of the " gold brick."

Henry Rocher, Photographer, Chicago, Ill.

AMERICAN PORTRAITURE TWENTY-FIVE YEARS AGO.

CHAPTER XII.

INCIDENTAL LIGHTING.

As the dawn comes out of darkness to awaken the day, so comes the faculty of observation and noting. What had been a blank takes form and definiteness. I began to see faces of men, women and children differently than I had done. I began to observe. It did not occur to me that I should do it, but gradually it came to be a habit and was resolved into a study. A pleasant, interesting, and, finally, a c o n s t a n t study. What one sees that may be helpful in his business or profession to adopt and store away for future needs are really additions to his capital. My study was to note how light fell upon the face and how the shadows were made. I q u i c k l y recognized and accepted what seemed correct and desirable, at the same time rejecting the incorrect. I was always seeking and adapting good lighting for portraits. That portion of the

Frank R. Bill, Photographer, Cleveland, O.

YOUNG RANCHMAN.

human world one sees is an open school — every face is a lesson offered gratuitously. The study is never a task, but always a pleasure, pursued without effort and unconsciously — an unceasing habit. Where could be found a study of such interest as the human face and head? Of the millions who people the earth, no two are exactly alike, a distinctive character to each.   A man does not necessarily wear a wart upon his nose to be distinguished from other men.   The wonder of God's creation could hardly be more significant than in this particular.   Nature has stamped its trade-mark on every human face. Students in physiognomy, who study deeply and sincerely, scrutinize faces more thoroughly than do other men.   The evil passions of brutal, hardened hearts, the vengeful spirit, the treacherous vindictive spite, the flashing eyes, the corrugated brow, the compressed lip, the expanding nostril, the clenched jaw, the murderous thought, are indexed in the faces of some; as also the generous, sympathetic, kindly promptings, the pleasant eye, the beaming smile, the welcoming spirit which springs out to meet and greet, are found in the faces of others.   Wonderful study, truly.   We find the rascal and hypocrite to be a poor imitation of a true and manly man.   I found my models in men at their desks, behind counters, in cars, in church, at the work-bench — wherever there was light and people, there was my school.   In the office of the business man at his desk, while discussing a trivial or important matter, I note how the light falls upon his face.   I note from whence it comes, how it is distributed.   I adapt the lighting for a portrait.   If, unconsciously, he turn his head toward or from the source, he gives me a more or less desirable change in the distribution and blending of shadows.   He is my model and my study.   He is posing to me without knowing it.   The child with whom I am making friends, whether he be shy or fearless, in the innocence of his little heart as he looks up, down or askance, has given me a pose and expression which delights me and which in my mind is transferred to the camera.   The stranger I meet upon the street who inquires for the City Hall has given me a hasty sitting.   I quite liked his face — while asking me a common question he was doing me a great service.   Like Dickens' " little Jenny Wren " I was always " trying on," and have a collection of mind images too great to be catalogued, and yet the work goes steadily on.   It gives the student valuable training.   This study has led me to observation beyond the camera, or its application to photography, and is in line of interest to the ladies.   Nature says they are of the gentler and softer sex; endowed with finer sensibilities, gentler and sweeter natures, more sympathetic and more refined.   Without venturing to dispute so great an authority we admit the claim and accede to it.   We recognize in women the

J. H. Garo, Photographer, Boston, Mass.

HER PORTRAIT.

cream of God's creation. From the cradle to the grave she is our
dearest blessing. The little breathing bud in her cradle holds our
hearts in her tiny hands, — she is our princess, we her slave. The
" wee tot " who runs to meet us with merry heart, and gives us
welcome to our home, is the brightest sunshine and our sweetest
pleasure — bless her! The maiden sweet and shy just realizing that
she has a heart; trusting, innocent, pure, honors her father and her
mother — bless her dear heart. The wife, the mother, the true
woman, the maker of a happy home, faithful, loyal, unselfish — bless
her noble heart. The dear old grandmother in her easy chair,
sweet in her lavender and laces; proud of her great brood of three
generations; full of stories for the children; loved by all, seeing
heaven plainer as she nears it — bless her dear old heart.

To such as these should come only the eider-down of kindness,
the soft breath of laden fields — all that contributes to harmony
should be theirs. Instead of rough winds, the gentle breeze.
Rather than a blaze of light, a soft subdued illumination, a light
which is mixed with shadow, a kindly mellow light, ladies, is best
for you — the soft light conceals what a harsh or brilliant light dis-
closes. Few people pay attention to or make a study of light and
lighting. As " there are sermons in stones," there are also lessons
in the shadow of a hitching-post. Knowledge and ignorance go
hand in hand. Light is both an enemy and a friend, according as
it may be used. We know it comes from the heavens rather than
out of the ground, yet choose to force it up hill rather than take it
first hand from the Creator. The manner of admitting light into
buildings and homes is faulty in the sense of giving best effects.
Windows should be high in rooms and light admitted through the
upper portions, rather than the lower. Rooms should be filled with
soft light to give cheer and health. Instead of dark or opaque
shades and heavy thick hangings, through which light can hardly
struggle, pleasant buff shades which are luminous and convey light,
aided by muslin or lace curtains, are best for homes. Shades hung
to pull up from the bottom rather than down from above are prefer-
able. As a rule, valuable pictures are given the gloom of hanging
space, while the floors are given the light. Dark wall papers are
depressing, while lighter tints and colors impart cheer and buoyancy.
Ladies may look to advantageous lighting as a means of enhancing
beauty. Keep in mind that a strong light produces violent contrast
of shadow and illumination which is trying to a lady's face. A soft
light and soft shadow gives gentle rounding and good definition —

concealing rather than empha-
sizing a possible blemish. In
sitting at a window the light
should pass a little in front of
the face and at an angle which
would admit of its reaching
the shaded side. To sit with a
strong light coming squarely
in front where both cheeks are
equally illuminated is to be
positively avoided. It makes
the face a blank by robbing it
of all shadows. The little
depressions and articulations of
surface anatomy are lost, while
a little turning of the head
either way immediately restores
the shadows by the changed
direction of light, and the lost
dimples, the contour of cupid's
bow to the lips, and little " well
holes " at corners of mouth, are
all back again. A judicious
blending of light with shadow
quickly makes or unmakes
beauty in a woman's face.
With an understanding of these
light and shadow values it is
as easy for ladies to look their
best as to fail in it. The
demonstration of this knowledge is easily acquired. The
reward comes quickly and satis-
factorily. In choosing a pew in

A MAN OF THE WORLD.

church it should be remembered that a window just opposite and
near the sitting is objectionable to good light effect — a seat or two
back is more desirable, as it avoids the abrupt shadow. Artificial
light, gas or electric, should be shaded with porcelain or ground glass.
The most favorable direction for the light to fall upon the person is
at the angle of forty-five degrees from above and ten to twenty
degrees back of the falling light. Do not try to abolish shadows,

but to soften them. Find the soft effects and wear them if you would
be lovely. An instance in illustration of the quality of light and the
direction in which it may fall upon a face may be understood by the
following description. A lady noted for her beauty — a brunette,
with soft dark eyes and clear fine complexion — spent an evening in
my house, to meet some friends whom I had prepared to see a
beautiful woman. It so happened that unconsciously she took a seat
directly under the chandelier where the force of light struck forehead,
nose, and cheeks, illuminating them abnormally. The shadows, by
violent contrast, quite concealed her eyes, leaving only black
patches of shade, with no illumination to give detail or expression.
The nose threw a heavy shadow across the upper lip, the mouth
and upon the chin; the lower portion of the cheeks, the throat and
neck, were in deep shadow. The lines at the corners of the mouth
were elongated and inky in shadow. There was a really handsome
woman looking absolutely hideous. Every smile she gave was a
grimace, a smooth skin was roughened, her hair was like wires. I
was greatly embarrassed at the injustice done her by an unscrupu-
lous light; hurriedly called my wife aside; directed her attention to
the unfortunate situation, and got her assistance in remedying without exposing it. When on some pretense she got the lady to rise I
hastily removed her chair to a position in a good light where justice
was done her and my friends were enabled to see her to advantage.
That women are not all alike, and their acts sometimes seem unaccountable, I offer this following incident in evidence. A woman about
forty, quiet and unobtrusive even to meekness, came in one day to
sit for a picture, but was quite undecided as to the style she ought
to have. She desired me to advise her if she had better have her
bonnet and shawl on, and whether she should have her hands to
show in the picture. I advised her as well as I could and we passed
into the sky-light room for the sitting. It happened that I had a
silver bath, which is a solution of nitrate of silver, in an evaporat-
ing dish upon a gas stove, being gently heated for the purpose of
purification. The solution in the porcelain dish was colorless and
clear like pure water. It struck me as I saw the woman step up to
the mirror and pick up a hair brush preparatory to redressing her
hair that I had better caution her against dipping the bristles into
the solution, so I called her attention to it and told her to avoid
touching it in any way, as it was a chemical under process of purification and would turn anything black that it came in contact with.
The dish was eight or ten feet from the dressing table and would

S. L. Cassar, Photographer, Valetta, Malta.

THEATRE ROYAL, VALETTA, MALTA.

seem safe from interference without the caution I gave. While she was fixing her hair I stepped into the reception room to meet a customer. On returning to my sitter she said, " Why, that water is warm; what did you tell me about it?" " I told you that it would color anything black that it came in contact with. Now, what have you done?" She replied, " I only wet the corner of the towel and wiped my face with it. Did you tell me it would turn me black?" The poor woman seemed to be just coming to a realization of her blunder, and was greatly excited. She said, " If you hadn't told me anything about that confounded stuff I wouldn't have thought of touching it. Oh, what shall I do? I'm in an awful state of mind." I explained to her that her face would turn black from her washing it with the chemical and would remain so for several days, until it gradually wore off; that it could only be removed by application of a deadly poison, which I dared not use; that she could not scour it off, but must patiently wait. I think I was as badly frightened as was the woman, and very anxious to get her home. I hurriedly went to a store, got some brown veiling, folded it double over her face, called a carriage and escorted her to her home.

I found her daughter and explained the mishap into which her mother had placed herself and got away as quickly as possible. I never heard a word of the lady afterward. She " kept dark," at least for a time, and I have, until now. I have always wondered what possessed the woman to disregard my caution and commit such a folly.

W. H. Partridge, Photographer, Boston, Mass.

FLOWER GIRL.

CHAPTER XIII.

TO CLEVELAND.

Evan D. Evans, Photographer, Ithaca, N. Y.

A STRIKING LIKENESS.

To replenish my stock of materials used in likeness work, I made occasional trips to Cleveland, and always called at Mr. Johnson's gallery, in the hope of meeting the man who lived in my mind as possessing the high standard of photography, but was never so fortunate as to find him. One day, to my surprise, he came into my rooms at the Beebe House, in Elyria, to find me, and, as he soon advised me, to secure my services as operator and manager of his business in Cleveland. He was opening a studio in New Orleans, where he would remain through the winter, and paid me the great compliment of offering me a position to step into his Cleveland establishment to take charge; to represent him until the following spring. I was really dazed that by so prominent a man as Mr. Johnson I should be considered competent to fill a position of such importance. I doubted my ability and candidly avowed it, but he encouraged me to believe I could fill the requirement. So, with some timidity and much pride, I accepted. I was a very happy young man because so fortunate an incident should fall in my way. It was an advance beyond my wildest dreams, and ambitious young fellows dream pretty wildly sometimes. Now, instead of the limited facilities of outfit that I carried in a packing trunk — even though it were a large one — from village to town, in my practice up to this time, I was to step into an established studio, having permanent fixtures and furnishings upon a liberal scale. A city gallery, with fine accessories and surroundings. Here I would have, too, fine examples of work to study. I would be taken out of a field and transplanted into a garden of richer soil. When I told Park I had engaged with Mr. Johnson for his Cleveland studio, and was soon to go, he, more than any other person in Elyria, could understand my exultation, and rejoiced with me. This move meant promotion to him also. He would take charge of the Elyria studio and stand in a similar relation to me that I did to Mr. Johnson. Like other beginners, having an ambition to progress, Park and I talked over the little we knew and the much we desired to learn in the daguerreotype art. I imparted to him what I could of my superior knowledge, and together we coveted the finish of the New York artists, for that city seemed the vortex of all excellence. New York, we fancied, showed a smarter style of finish than any other American city, and we had the hardihood to fancy we might hope some day to come within a day's ride of New York quality. A country tailor likes to see a Broadway coat. In the same sense a daguerreotype man may take a lesson. Park wished to learn of me the names of the most prominent men conducting the business in the principal cities. He was desirous of visiting the noted establishments to see the best achievements of the camera in skilled hands — a common wish, but few can compass its indulgence. We would sometimes see, in the hands of people from larger cities, examples of work bearing a metropolitan air, and smarter style. These we would carefully study. They were our chance opportunities, always welcome; our " pickings by the wayside," never to be neglected. I was somewhat familiar with the work of some of the New York establishments, but could not make him see from my description, as I could remember from having seen; but felt confident we would go to New York together sometime and have a good look. Coming back to the point of former question as to whom I considered the ablest picture man in New York, I said, " Well, Charley, there are many prominent daguerreotypists in that city — some in a particular way in advance of others, and it is difficult to discriminate. I think Brady stands at the head as to prominence. He has studios in New York and Washington. He has taken portraits of more public and prominent people than any of his rivals. Presidents, senators, governors, congressmen, ambassadors, statesmen of all degrees, notables of all countries have sat to him. He has made a point of securing portraits of notables, and

Geo. J. Rogers, Photographer, Albany, N. Y.

A TYPE OF JOHNNY BULL.

has the largest collection extant. His name is synonymous with photography. Fredericks, too, is prominent. He has the most imposing of the New York establishments. He has also a fine establishment in Havana, Cuba, and divides his time between the two cities. He has brought from Paris some fine artists for finishing portraits in oils and pastels. He has a large business. Gurney is also a prominent figure in New York as a photographer. He has made a great success. Bogardus, Plum, Lawrence, Root Brothers, of New York and Philadelphia; Meade Brothers, of New York and Albany, are all prominent for ability, and have made marks for themselves." "Well, who are the best in Boston?" continued Park. I replied: "As to who is best I can hardly venture to say. The names of Whipple, Black, Southworth and Marshall stand prominent." "Now give us Philadelphia," says Park. "M. A. Root, Broadbent, McClees and Germon, I have heard, are most prominent. Baltimore — Whitehurst, who has also a branch in Washington. Cincinnati — Fontayne & Porter, Faris, Hawkins. Chicago — Fassett, Cook, Hessler, Shaw. St. Louis — Fitz Gibbon, Cramer, Scholten, Fox. Buffalo — Evans and Powelson, and that, Charley, is about the extent of notables as far as I know." He carefully wrote in a memorandum book the names of the cities and men for future reference. On going to Cleveland to familiarize myself with the place and its workings, I felt like an overgrown boy entering a strange school. I met there John Killerbine, a German boy of eighteen, who had been assistant to Mr. Johnson four years and was, for a boy, quite proficient. I saw readily from John's mental measure of me that I was, in his estimation, just a country daguerreotype taker, and could never fill Mr. Johnson's shoes. The serious task of living that impression down was before me. This daguerreotype establishment was located in the Merchants' Bank building, corner of Superior and Bank streets, and opposite the Weddell House, the most central location and the busiest corner in the city at that time. It was the foremost gallery and had the best patronage. My earnest efforts to please were understood and generally appreciated. A bright business man told me one day he had always noticed "molasses caught more flies than vinegar," adding, "your best capital is in your polite and genial manners; of course you'll succeed." I knew the wisdom of his remark before he gave it to me, but his manner of saying it impressed me. I never lost sight of that excellent business rule. Many a time when I have been "sore tried" by an overexacting and what seemed an unreasonable customer, and anger rising, I have turned to the molasses and "won out." Cleveland, at that time, with but about twenty thousand population, and holding her head pretty high as being the metropolis of northern Ohio, was, as compared with the present, 1902, with a population of four hundred and fifty thousand, simply in her swaddling clothes. There was not a paved street, and but few paved sidewalks in her corporate limits. No water supply except from dug wells and rain cisterns. The water we used in the performance of our business was carried in buckets from the canal, a distance of a quarter of a mile, which was cheerfully spanned by Killerbine, who, with a bucket in each hand, brought enough

JIM.

for our stoneware jar to last us a week.

"COULD YOU LOVE ME?"

Nowadays a hundred gallons a day is used by each photographic establishment of any pretension. The sand in the streets from four to six inches deep made hard pulling for horses with vehicles. Our first paving was of plank, which, as an improvement upon the sand road of Superior street, was a matter of pride and rejoicing. As it wore down it took on something of an elastic condition, and the rubbing together of the edges wore spaces between, so that, after a smart rain, rapid driving, where water was collected under the planks, would force up the slush through the cracks as high as a horse's back.

Euclid street was, at that

time, an exclusive resident street — not avenue yet — peopled by the *crème de la crème*. Noble mansions of the rich, the proud — because they had the right to be; the kindly and good, because it was their natures. The sun which sent its friendly rays to illume and beautify the mansion and throw shadows of shrubs and trees across the beautifully kept lawn, reached also the figure of a poor pinched woman with basket upon her arm and little girl grasping the skirt of faded dress, while eating from the other hand the bounty of the kitchen as they pass out through the driveway. It is good to be rich. It is good that the rich know charity. Euclid street was filled — not closely filled, with residences. Not a shop or a store upon it. It was the road to Doan's Corners out Euclid way. I gave myself the pleasure many times of loitering past those beautiful homes and admiring them to my heart's content. I thanked the proprietors mentally and heartily for the pleasure they gave me. They were not building for me; but I seemed able to admire and recognize the beautiful, possibly in a measure equal to themselves. I could go every day; take in new draughts of pleasure, and as I drifted homeward could hug myself with the thought that while I could enjoy as much as the other fellow, he had to pay the taxes. It was but a short distance east from the Public Square — perhaps two miles — where rail fences in zig-zag pattern bordered the highway and a toll-gate barred the passage of teams, demanding tribute for road repairs. Farms and land could be bought by the acre then, while now it is sold by the foot front, and palatial homes jostle each other and vie for supremacy in beauty and splendor. It is Euclid avenue now, and reaches for miles through city, hamlet, village and township, and the echo of its name reaches over the world where, with other noted streets, it is mentioned and recognized. While " progress " has elbowed our original friend " off the track," we still recognize in it beauty and merit which have not to this day been surpassed.

I was getting along. We pushed our way through the winter slowly and surely. At Christmas time we were more than usually busy in doing our share for the happy season of gifts, in which a handsomely encased likeness played a good part. Again at Easter we were well patronized. Compare these days with later times — the light expenditures for salaries and materials, the good prices we received for our products, the ease with which we could and did take from $10 to $20 and even $50 per day, one man and one boy, all the work of the day finished and delivered — the cash for same in the safe, as a rule. No coming back in the evening to wash or mount prints, no proofs to prepare, no varnishing, sacking up and filing away negatives. The evenings without care or work — indeed, the golden days of photography seem to be back forty or fifty years ago, under the name of daguerreotype.

H. H. Pierce, Photographer, Providence, R. I.

A DAUGHTER OF EGYPT.

CHAPTER XIV.

GROWTH.

I remember on awakening one sleepy Sunday afternoon, my room darkened by heavy green paper shades, closely rolled down, my surprise at seeing upon the wall at the foot of my bed — on a clean, whitewashed wall, a miniature cow walking leisurely along, every motion, even to the swish of her tail, as natural as possible. I could not account for it — the image was distinct and clear. She was walking upside down, her feet toward the ceiling of the room and her back toward the floor. I wondered if I could be dreaming, or from what the illusion could be caused. I had never seen or heard of such a manifestation before. I hurriedly got off the bed to investigate, pulled the curtain aside and looked out upon the street — there was the cow moving contentedly along unmindful of the exhibition she had given me or the mystery I was in about her. She had demonstrated the principle of the camera obscura and of pinhole photography. There was, as I found, a hole the size of a pin-head through the paper shade, located near the center, through which had been carried the image of " bossy " as through a lens. The reversal of the image I was conversant with from the use of the camera, and by it was helped to an understanding of the upside-down cow phenomenon. I knew so little and there was so much to learn I studied diligently. I studied and dreamed, was always wondering what might be the future for the young art of photography. I wondered if it might ever happen that portrait heads the size of life would be made with a camera — wondered if the Voigtländer family would develop a giant which might compass such a feat.

Looking back to those days of my wonderings, and comparing them with the present, it all seems like a fairy story.

Infants which were brought to me for daguerreotypes in turn brought their own infants and again their grandchildren. I have taken groups of four generations, the individual members of which I had taken singly along in the years since 1850. The discovery of Daguerre was indeed a blessing to humanity. It brought the

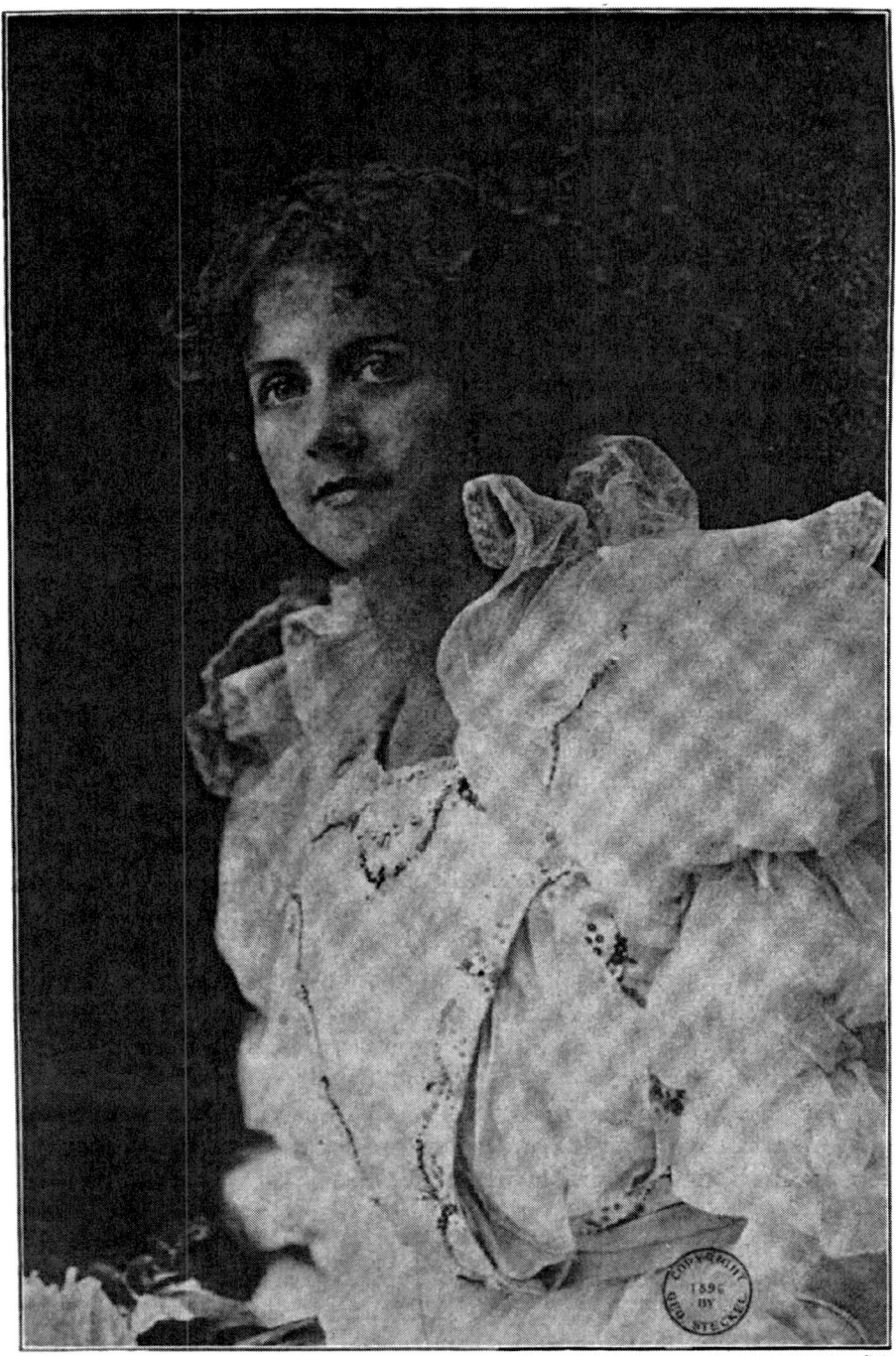

Geo. Steckel, Photographer, Los Angeles, Cal.

EMMA BEACH YAW, PRIMA DONNA.

true likeness of our friends into our homes — into our very hands. The little tot with blond hair, with serious or smiling face, who from boyhood had grown, is now the substantial man of affairs, or perhaps has been gathered to his fathers. The little maid in the bread-and-butter period of life, braids her hair down each shoulder, with her doll or kitten in her arms, who knows naught of a wicked world, goes to school with her first reader and her slate; she comes home hungry and gets her slice of bread and butter spread with sugar, the child without care, the confiding, affectionate, demure little " mouse of the cupboard," is now the mother, possibly the grand-mother of some one who loves that old daguerreotype. The thou-sands of likenesses of fathers, mothers, brothers and sisters stored carefully away in bureau drawers to be taken out and looked at, to awaken recollections, to stir hearts and sometimes start tears, the tender histories twining about them, the untold value of the precious keepsakes, all stand in evidence of the worth of the blessed discovery. I recall an instance of a gentleman who, many years ago, brought in to have copied a picture of a little boy who had passed out of earth life. He impressed upon me the requirement of great care. " Let nothing happen to that picture," he said, " all the gold in California could not buy it." I assured him that I would take the greatest care that no harm came to it. I kept it carefully locked in my safe. I felt he had entrusted me with a responsibility that was burdensome, because of the great value he attached to the picture. I was anxious he should call and take it away. Some days after I had the copy completed and ready for delivery I met him on the street, and very glad I was to see him. I told him his little boy's picture was ready for him and I wanted him to call and get it. He said, " Yes, I will call to-morrow," and added, " Nothing has happened to the original picture? You are sure, for all the gold in California could not buy it." I assured him the picture was all right, rejoicing to myself that it was to be delivered on the morrow.

He did not happen to come. It was several weeks before I saw him again — this time, as before, on the street. I stopped him and told him again I was very anxious to deliver that picture. He said he had been quite busy and I must excuse him, but he would be in to-morrow *sure* and get it.

I suppose he must have been very busy again, for he did not come. As the years passed by and the picture was occasionally picked up and examined while looking for some other one, we all,

WHERE THE POND-LILIES GROW.

my employes as well as myself, grew to know it as surpassing in value "all the gold in California." In the course of time we got quite an accumulation of such pictures, which the owners "would call for again," but none whose value quite approached the little boy's.

Daguerre planted the seed of practical and valuable photography. It had swelled, sprouted and burst through into the light and was reaching for growth. Scientific investigators bent friendly gazes upon it, patted it upon the head in encouragement, watered its roots, and fertilized the soil surrounding and sustaining it. A promising, hardy shrub it had grown to be, and was destined to bear good fruit upon branches springing from a noble trunk.

It offered to students in science a fascinating pleasure and interest. Like a child who wearies with a toy, many who treated it as a plaything dropped it for more congenial pursuits, while others who got their fingers stained in earnest stuck to it and became photographers.

Now came a step in evolution. We were soon to lay aside present methods and formulas for a radical departure to a presumable improvement. Scott Archer, of England, a prominent scientific investigator and experimentalist, discovered and introduced collodion as a vehicle in which to form and carry the photographic image upon a plate of glass instead of a plate of copper faced with silver, as had been practiced by all followers of Daguerre from the time of his discovery-invention.

In the daguerreotype the sensitive principle was secured and produced as has been described in foregoing pages, by vapors of iodine and bromine uniting and combining upon the silver surface plate. In the production of a negative or an ambrotype by means of collodion each step in the process was made by the employment of fluids, while the principle of sensitive creation and chemical phenomena, bromo-iodide of silver, were identical, the means of production were different from the daguerreotype. For every likeness made, a separate and distinct sitting was required. A person wanting a number of likenesses for distribution had quite a task in securing them.

I remember when Jenny Lind sang in Cleveland, Mr. Johnson secured a sitting of her. The demand for her pictures was large and the original daguerreotype had to be copied one at a time for all these pictures. It was a part of my work to do them. I made quite an acquaintance with her in the performance of this daily work.

The advantage of adopting the negative plate as a substitute was, that on securing a successful image from the sitter or any object to be taken, there could be reproduced upon paper any number of prints desired, thus saving the presence of the sitter and the avoidance of imposing a heavy task upon him. Just think of it! Why, the sitter might be in an adjoining state and we be printing pictures of him in his absence. Gracious goodness! What are we coming to? It may come to pass yet that pictures be taken of people without their knowing or suspecting it. Surely we are in an age of progress and astonishments.

The collodion problem was undergoing experiments in the hands of scientists and experts abroad. The American photographer is indebted largely to his European brother for much of his knowledge and progress — the European is interested and more patient as an investigator. By his patience, thoroughness and diligence he accomplishes in his own time and way what the "hurry up"

American abandons too readily. We get from Europe much which has been patiently worked out and proven by the discoverer or adapter. We get things ready made. We sometimes pick up the thread in the seam where our patient cousin was taking a rest, and make a push to oust him.

P. S. Ryder, Photographer, Syracuse, N. Y.

YOUNG MADONNA.

CHAPTER XV.

COLLODION.

Collodion is a mixture of alcohol and ether in which is dissolved guncotton, the addition of which changes it from the most limpid fluid to a glutinous, slow-flowing substance resembling syrup.

In the collodion is introduced a soluble iodide and bromide. In preparing to make a negative or positive image, the collodion is flowed over a carefully cleansed plate of glass and the excess is drained from the plate back into the bottle from which it was poured. The alcohol and ether being very volatile, evaporate quickly, leaving a coating like a heavy varnish upon the plate. The plate is now immersed, by means of a forked rod upon which it is placed, into a solution of nitrate of silver, held in a bath vessel especially constructed for the purpose, and immediately the silver in solution is attracted to the iodide and bromide in the collodion film, changing the latter from a colorless condition to a cream white, which is the sensitive principle, bromo-iodide of silver. This preparation must be made in a darkened room, else the light would destroy the sensitiveness of the film upon the plate. After the exposure of the plate in the camera on the sitter, it is returned to the dark room and developed by flooding it with a solution of sulphate of iron. It is an interesting part of the process to watch the image rise from the film from apparent nothingness to the reality of a truthful likeness of a person.

The ambrotype came as the first product of collodion in photography. It was a departure from, yet resembling the daguerreotype, being a case picture, taken upon glass instead of the silver surface plate. The mirror-like surface of the polished daguerreotype plate was abolished in the ambrotype and the image more readily seen, a pleasant change and welcome improvement.

Mr. S. D. Humphrey, of Canandaigua, New York, started a journal of photography, calling it *Humphrey's Journal*. To be able to hurl it with greater impetus from a central point, he went to New York City and established his publication office and headquarters. I subscribed for *Humphrey's Journal* and continued a subscriber as long as it lasted. There was another magazine, under the title of *Photographic and Fine Art Journal*, by H. H. Snelling, also of New York City. To this I also subscribed and continued during its life of several years. From these journals I read of collodion and the advantages which would result from its introduction. I opened correspondence with Mr. Humphrey, with reference to introducing the ambrotype in Cleveland, and asked for the address of a competent instructor. He offered to come himself, provided I could secure him a class that would justify it. I quickly had a class

A DINNER PARTY.

of ten, at $100 each, of photographers from surrounding towns and cities who were anxious to be instructed. We wanted to drink from the fountain-head and were satisfied; from Mr. Humphrey we got the sparkle and foam as well as the real body. He gave us careful instructions and a fine start. I desired to hold Cleveland exclusively to myself for as long a time as I could in the new picture, and was rewarded with a fine business by holding the control.

The ambrotype was a very popular picture. While inferior to the daguerreotype, in fact it was something new, it took a smart run and practically extinguished the daguerreotype. To overcome the effect of the transparency of the glass and give solidity to the collodion image, it was necessary to coat the glass with asphaltum — black varnish — which in time would crack and flake off the glass. A remedy for this and a shorter cut to the work was the introduction of the so-called tintype, which, in turn, superseded the picture upon glass, and has shown wonderful vitality. Pleasure resorts without them would seem a hollow mockery. In both styles, the daguerreotype and ambrotype, a separate sitting was required for every picture made.

The next step in progress was to produce the negative image, from which could be multiplied prints to any extent upon especially prepared paper. While the negative print was produced with collodion upon a glass plate, the method was varied; the image was made to obstruct the light from passing through. It was to be seen and judged of by transmitted instead of reflected light. The production of the negative is a much more difficult process, requiring more certain skill, bringing more routine processes, and dividing or classifying the work into departments, and requiring additional persons to be employed in the production of a photographic print. The negative required at least six handlings before being ready for printing, and the paper from start to finish required, through the different stages of process and handling, fifteen manipulations. This additional handling necessitated the employment of more dishes, trays, bottles, more room in which to work and more people. It will be seen the advance to progress was attended with expense and imposed study and work to master the new methods, some of which seemed crooked, capricious and difficult.

'Tis said " the course of true love does not run smooth," the whims of a balky horse are unaccountable, the freaks of chemicals are mysterious; the " disagreements " between a new batch of collodion and an untried silver bath are worthy subjects for a divorce court. The hand which can smooth them to a condition of harmony often scratches the roof of a puzzled brain, and strokes a non-committal beard many a time and oft. It may be a running fight between them for days, when at length a morning may dawn upon the discord, and with joined hands they move along harmoniously together without the photographer knowing which had been to blame.

Now for a time I return to Elyria to inaugurate the ambrotype and teach my " understudy " the mysteries of collodion. Elyria seemed more my home. To get back there among my old friends was very enjoyable. Park welcomed me back right heartily. His progress during my absence had been most satisfactory. I was quite surprised at the skill he had developed in so short a time.

My few months in Cleveland had brightened me, as was evident to us both. Park was anxious to transfer some of my Cleveland " shine " to himself, and together we coveted the greater polish of New York, for to us that city was the vortex of supremacy in picture achievements.

LITTLE JIM AND HIS OLD GRAY HORSE.
In one Canto (Canter).

Have you seen Little Jim and his Old Gray Horse,
Starting out on a jaunt to " Banbury Cross?"
He is sitting astride of his Gran'pa's neck,
And is pulling his hair, his antics to check:
With a determinate mien he's clucking along,
Or else, peradventure, he's singing this song. —

I love Gran'pa and he loves me,
And ain't we cute as cute can be?
I'm " Little Jim " and he's the " Horse,"
And we're going to " Banb'ry Cross."

E. HEINRICHS.

CHAPTER XVI.

PHOTOGRAPHIC ASSOCIATIONS.

A convention of several hundred photographers met in New York City, at the Cooper Institute, April 7, 1868, to take measures for resisting what was alleged, and finally proven to be, an unjust patent granted to James A. Cutting, of Boston, Mass., for the employment of bromides in collodion. This patent was very burdensome to photographers, as a heavy tax was imposed upon all who used collodion. Mr. Edward L. Wilson, publisher of the Philadelphia *Photographer*, at Philadelphia, was elected to manage the contest; testimony was taken in Philadelphia and Boston covering a period of six months; many witnesses were examined. The case was argued in Washington, D. C., before the Commissioner of Patents, and the patentee was defeated. This was mainly accomplished by the testimony of Jex Bardwell, of Detroit, Mich., whose verbal and documentary evidence was so comprehensive and clear that victory was declared for the photographers. The New York convention was adjourned to meet the following year at Philadelphia, where was organized the " National Photographers' Association," whose objects and aims were

C. F. Conly, Photographer, Boston, Mass.
"DO YOU WANT TO KISS ME GOODNIGHT?"

PORTRAIT.

protection from unjust patents; for annual conventions and exhibitions; for mutual improvement and interchange of ideas, in an educational direction. This association proved of great value and gave a healthy growth to the art. It continued several years, meeting in various cities, when at the Centennial Exposition in 1876 at Philadelphia the general attractions were so great as to overshadow our modest efforts and the association took a rest. In 1880 a new association was formed at Chicago, under the name of " The Photographers' Association of America," which has proven so vigorous that now, in 1902, its twenty-second meeting is quite equal to any former one. At the initial meeting at Chicago, was made the first public demonstration of the bromo-gelatine dry plate, by Mr. John Carbutt, of Philadelphia, the pioneer manufacturer of dry plates in America. I was present at his demonstration, which was made at the studio of A. J. Copelin. So eager were all to see the plates developed that the dark room in which the work was done was packed by at least twenty persons, although it was not possible for more than two or three, besides Mr. Carbutt, to witness the process. To us, who were accustomed to seeing collodion plates developed in two or three minutes, the requirement of ten to fifteen minutes to develop and " fix " a gelatine dry plate seemed a tiresome process. Since 1855 various persons by various methods have experimented in efforts to produce dry plates. Some were successful, but in all cases were impractical, because of a lack of sensitiveness to give rapidity of action. They were all too slow until gelatine was discovered to give greater rapidity and was adopted and perfected. Dr. Richard Leach Maddox, of Edinburgh, was the inventor of the gelatine-bromide dry plate, in 1871. Then a new impetus was given, as the introduction of the gelatine dry plate in photography was the most important step in advancement since 1880. It revolutionized and simplified the most difficult part of the work in negative making; it " let down the bars " to the photographic world, so that all could enter a new field which offered pleasure, occupation, and education. By the collodion, or so-called " wet process," the operator must necessarily be conversant with chemistry, and carefully exercise such knowledge in his daily — his hourly-work, as the preparation of his plate was a question of skill, guided by chemical judgment, to secure fine effects. In the dry plate the qualities necessary to uniform excellence were put in the plate in its manufacture at the factory. A person without musical knowledge can turn the crank of a hand organ, and get results; a novice can " press a button " and, with the assistance of the man who " does the rest," become a photographer — *in his mind.* The dry plate sounded the signal for kodaks and other instantaneous cameras with odd and significant names which sprang up like mushrooms, making their bows to multitudes of amateur photographers. Now, through meadows, over hills, beside running brooks and broad waters, in grazing fields among cattle and

Henry S. Williams, Photographer, Philadelphia.

" MY SHEEP HEAR MY VOICE."

sheep, through familiar lanes, in shady wood, goes the man or woman for a new pleasure and a new study. They find, unobserved until now, beauties in shrub and tree, in stump and rock, in waving fields of growing grain, in picturesque stacks of harvested corn bordered by rail fences; they begin to note the value of shadows; nature speaks, is heard and recognized; she invites the eye to her beauty spots which before may have been regarded as blemishes; a moss-covered log going to decay in the silent woods; a fallen tree spanning a stream, are pictures. With a camera in hand, an artistic perception alert, there are pictures scattered about in profusion waiting to be garnered. The man or woman must learn to find and to *see* them, and so the camera is indeed a pleasure giver and educator. I had been a photographer a third of a century when the dry plate came. The romance and enthusiasm of so-called field work had, with me, quite sobered down. The carrying of apparatus, baths, trays, jugs of chemicals and water; setting up a tent for a dark room by the roadside or in the field was so much a discomfort that a carrying case filled with dry plates and camera on shoulder was a joy by contrast. I was as eager for "viewing" as any new beginner possibly could be, and the pleasure I found is beyond my ability to describe. Many people with art instinct have shown great work and possibilities with the camera, and many an object-lesson has the amateur given the professional photographer. The most conspicuous achievement in possibilities of dry plate work, and one that will stand for years to come, was given by Edward L. Wilson, Ph. D., of Philadelphia. Early in 1881 he made the tour of the Holy Land to gather material for his very complete and interesting book, " In Scripture Lands." To provide for reliable illustrations he went equipped for making photographic views, and for the purpose Mr. John Carbutt stocked him with carefully prepared plates. The trip extended up the Nile one thousand miles to the second cataract, on steamboat; to Mt. Sinai and Petra, in Arabia, on camels' backs — those "ships of the desert;" Palestine from south to north, all on horseback; the pyramids, monoliths, sphinxes, ruins of ancient cities, Jerusalem, the Red Sea, and the sea of Galilee; Nazareth, Bethlehem, Lebanon, Damascus — all the principal points of sacred and historic interest were visited and photographed. These plates, exposed to climatic changes, the heat of the desert, the moisture of sea voyages twice across, the penetrating salt and bilge evaporations very trying to delicate chemically prepared structures, carried the images cast upon them, through several months' duration, and were brought back to Philadelphia to the laboratory where they were prepared and the latent images aroused from their sleep, by the process of development, to objects of living interest. Mr. Wilson's success was of a character so phenomenally striking, as a demonstration favorable to the dry plate, that its value was then and there recognized. The world, photographic and otherwise, understands that it has been a factor of the highest value.

Edward L. Wilson, Ph. D., Photographer.

A GROUP OF BEDOUINS AT THE ENTRANCE TO THE GORGE OF THE
KUZNAH, PETRA, ARABIA.

CHAPTER XVII.

BURNED OUT AT ELYRIA.

Now it came to pass in the winter of 1852 that I was married to a sister of Park, which more closely cemented the friendship between us. Some three weeks after the marriage I was aroused from sleep early one morning before daylight, by heavy pounding upon the entrance door to the house. I recognized Park's voice calling out: " Hello! Get up! Were you insured? " I answered I was not. " Well," said he, " the block is burned to the ground. All is lost; the door to your gallery rooms was not even opened." That was uncomfortable news for a young couple just starting in life. I hurried over to see the ruins, which were not unlike other ruins by fire, but to me it meant much. I had just laid in a good stock of materials; all the best of my effects, even my clothing was gone, as my bachelor quarters, adjoining my gallery rooms, had not been removed — all was gone. *Voigtländer* was in the ruins. I was shocked and, in a manner, bereaved. This disaster gave me a chance to start even with the world again. A lot of friends gathered about me expressing sympathy and regret; urged me to " keep a stiff upper lip," and assuring me that they would do all they could to help me in a new start. I took the morning train for Cleveland to purchase a new outfit; as we went gliding along past farms, houses, and barns, crossing muddy roads occasionally, the disconsolate mood upon me shut all cheerfulness out of sight. It was not a pleasant morning; the outlook was dismal indeed. I had but a few dollars in my pocket, and I doubted whether the stock-house would give me credit for a new start; my mind was full. The " castle-in-the-air " cottage, with imagination as architect, had been mine, and had grown almost to material form by the aid of a creative mind; the porch which had been fashioned from a dream — that cozy porch, with vines climbing over it; inviting seats, with at times a tea-table spread there, where our friends could sit with us, sip their tea and praise the light biscuits of the young wife; where could be planned outings to the woods, and to the lake; to the seashore and the mountains; all these pleasant

C. W. Schide, Photographer, Elyria, O.
WEST BRANCH FALLS, ELYRIA, OHIO.

creations were rudely swept back to the regions of chaos from whence they had sprung, leaving me face to face with misfortune represented by ruins and bare walls, with all my earthly possessions smoldering in the mass in the basement of the block; as I had gazed long and sadly upon the scene a couple of hours before, and which possessed my mind, as though I were standing at the funeral pyre of my wrecked small fortune. At this point the Omnibus Company's agent calls out: "Baggage for Cleveland! Ride up in the bus; hotels, or any part of the city," and I am awakened to myself again, at the depot. I ran up a moment to see Mr. Johnson and Mr. Killerbine, who were very sorry for my loss, and hoped I would soon make it up again. Mr. Johnson called out to me as I was hurrying away, saying: "If you want anything that I can spare, you are welcome to it — and say, keep a stiff upper lip!" I thanked him, and crossed the street to the stock-house of Gaylord & Hammond, furnishers of photographic materials and instruments. I told Mr. Gaylord of my loss by fire, and that I had come to get a new outfit, mostly on credit. As I had small acquaintance with the house, Mr. Gaylord asked me if I could secure them for the indebtedness which I desired to make, and followed that question with another — " Have you got anything besides your clothes? " I informed him that I had not even clothing beyond what I had on; that all was lost in the fire. Perhaps it then occurred to him that it was a mistake to strike a man that was down, and he said, hurriedly: " Pardon me for asking that question, Mr. Ryder; I should not have done it." Continuing, he said: " Whatever you may need you can have credit for. I feel sure we shall not lose by you." I thanked him, and proceeded to make selection of goods. I found a twin brother to my lost Voigtländer, and, after a careful examination, adopted him as a substitute for the cremated member of his honorable family. I hurried back to Elyria the same night, and the following morning looked up a location for a new studio. I was fortunate in finding a suitable place and made all haste to occupy it. I put out a new sign, and hung empty frames, suggestive of my wiped-out-by-fire condition, at the stairway entrance; hurriedly made a few specimen pictures of well-known citizens, and engaged a young boy — now a substantial merchant of Cleveland — to go out as drummer for me. I got up a respectful and what was meant to be a sympathy-reaching circular, which, with my new-made specimens in a tastefully lined basket, my young hustler was turned loose upon the citizens. His mother had fixed him up " spick and span." I was really proud of him; he was a little gentleman from the ground up. It was his first business enterprise, and he was going into it to win. His instructions were to visit every home in the village; to show the pictures, and leave circulars. This work he did faithfully and thoroughly. I praised him; made him feel that his tact and diligence were appreciated. With eagerness he watched the results of his work; he came in often to report his visits, and to learn if those who had promised to call had done so. He was surely stirring up a business for me; was driving fish into my net. When he had well canvassed the village, I started him to go over the same ground again, and was well rewarded; he stirred up the tardy ones, was evidently doing our customers good service, and surely they were doing us the same. It was a lesson in business methods to me, as well as to my young representative. I gave him full credit for his share of the work; he was gratified to know he was really a power; he was proud to be so. He may be a better merchant today for having gained a bit of business experience in boyhood. In a very few months I had paid up all my obligations, and was in better financial condition than before.

CHAPTER XVIII.

MORNING RAMBLES.

In the mornings before business hours I took short journeys
of discovery to learn bearings and
main features of Cleveland. In
any direction it was not far to the
outskirts of the city, to the shores
of the lake, or to the river, and
good squirrel-shooting was close
at hand. The Public Square was
a fenced-in park, with openings
for pedestrians from the sidewalks at Superior and Ontario
streets, offering entrance to cows
as well as people, which offer was
promptly accepted by those lovers
of tender grass. A divided opinion existed in the minds of the
people as to the propriety of putting fences across the streets,
compelling people in vehicles to
drive around, rather than straight
through. Ladies would stand
aside, giving precedence to the
honest bossys at the obstruction
posts which prevented vehicles
passing through, and, on occasion,
stepped higher than usual in passing those points. Mr. Irad Kelley, a prominent and eccentric
citizen of those days, believed the
park to be reserved ground and
not an open highway for teams.
So it happened on occasional

H. H. Pierce, Providence, R. I.

THE GIPSY QUEEN.

pleasant mornings, after a period of open highways, that the
sun would rise upon a fenced-in park, and Mr. Kelley, of
Euclid street, would seem exultant, while other citizens would
frown.   Doctor Ackley, also a prominent citizen, entertaining views
opposed to the closed park, seeing Mr. Kelley on a morning after
a fencing-in of the Square, asked him if he purposed sowing
his lot to buckwheat.   Mr. Kelley replied in a high tenor
peculiar to himself, employing language that produced an abnormal
heat at the back of the doctor's neck, and for weeks they passed
each other on opposite sides of the street.   It would happen again
while Mr. K. was enjoying healthful slumbers and dreams of having his own sweet way and the pleasure of driving around the park
rather than through it, that he would find on coming down town
that the sections of fence obstructions had been removed; had
vanished in the night.   To the indifferent citizen — who had no
horse to drive, other than his foot on which to trot his children,
and to trot himself to the shop, with his basket on his arm each
morning — this matter of " now you see it, and now you don't,"
as concerned the park system of a future great city, did not seriously disturb him.

Passing up Superior street on the southwest corner of the
Square was the Dunham House—now the Forest City Hotel.   Immediately in front, in the southwest section of the Public Square,
was the court house, and just back of it the jail.   Continuing
eastward on Superior street through the park, or Public Square,
on the right was the Hoffman Block, which had replaced the Mrs.
W. Lemon residence, and which in turn has been replaced by the
Cuyahoga Building.   On the opposite corner of Superior street and
the Public Square stood the residence of Leonard Case, Sr., with a
broad porch and heavy fluted columns.   Just north of that and
fronting the Public Square was " The Ark," a low building one
story in height.   It became a rendezvous for a number of young
men of social and congenial natures who would meet there in the
evenings.   There was no regularly organized club or association.
They were staid, scholarly men; had a library of rare books of
natural history and science, and the meetings were regulated by
the code of good sense and judgment, honor and benevolence;
always orderly, never boisterous; no banquets, and no bottles other
than those used for candlesticks which came in vogue because of a
misunderstanding with the Cleveland Gas Company.   A nightly
smoker was the only form of dissipation.   The building was called

THE FIRE-PLACE IN THE OLD ARK.

the " Ark," because the members of the assemblage which gathered there were disciples of Nimrod, and a fine collection of birds
and animals of their own capture were carefully taxidermied and set
up in glass cases, in the south end of the building, forming quite
a museum, and suggesting Noah's ancient water-craft. The men
who composed this unique society were: William Case, Leonard
Case, Jr., Stoughton Bliss, Capt. B. A. Stannard, Dr. Elisha Ster-
ling, James J. Tracy, Bushnell White, D. W. Cross, Geo. A. Stan-
ley, R. K. Winslow, H. G. Abbey, John Coon, E. A. Scovill, Rodney
Gale, Dr. A. Maynard, Levi T. Schofield.

When the United States government purchased the site for
Post-office, Custom House, and United States Court, the Ark was
moved across Wood street, just back of the City Hall, on the present
(1902) temporary site of the Public Library. The members continued to occupy it until the Case Library building was completed,
when Leonard Case, Jr., set apart for the " Arkites " two large rooms
in the southeast corner of the building on the third floor, to be theirs
to occupy so long as the last member should live. The surviving
members in 1902 are James J. Tracy and Levi T. Schofield of Cleveland, and John Coon of Kansas City, Missouri. Now that the
United States government has condemned the site of Case Library
building for the purpose of using it, together with that of the old
Post-office, for the new Federal building, which is to be erected on
a scale commensurate with the present population of 450,000, the
" Arkites " are without a home. The more valuable belongings of
the old society have been divided between the Western Reserve
Historical Society and Case School of Applied Science, the latter
having been founded by Leonard Case, Jr.

On the north side of Superior street where now stand the City
Hall, gas office, and business buildings, including the *Plain Dealer*
publishing establishment at corner of Bond street, there were very
few buildings. Mr. S. B. Axtell occupied a brick residence nearly
midway between Wood and Bond streets, and Mr. Edwin Shep-
herd's cottage, long and low, set well back toward Rockwell street,
with a broad, deep and fine garden extending quite to the picket
fence at the Superior street sidewalk; a gate opening in the center;
a broad gravel walk bordered with box, reaching back to the cottage,
formed one of the most noticeable places on that square. It was a
place at which to linger, and to admire. Continuing east of Bond
street were the residences of Philo Chamberlain, Henry Wick, W.
Corning, T. S. Beckwith, J. W. Gray, Sheldon Pease, and Augustus

Handy. Fronting Superior street on Erie, and standing upon what is now Superior street, was the "May Cottage," stretching out its wings upon the fine grounds and looking down Superior street as if to say, "No thoroughfare beyond me," and there ended Superior street. Coming west on the south side from the corner of Erie street we pass the residences of Edwin Cowles, Dr. J. P. Robinson, R. K. Winslow, Henry Chisholm, James Farmer, and S. A. Raymond, to what is now Bond street; but there was no street there at

F. C. Schumacher, Photographer, Los Angeles, Cal.

"WE'SE GWINE TO CUT A WATERMILION."

that time. We continue past Trinity Church, past residences and cottages back to the Public Square. Looking across to the north side of the Public Square, on the corner of Ontario street we see the first Presbyterian church, and there it stands yet, rebuilt from destruction by fire. On the corner opposite, where now stands the massive Society for Savings building, stood the Crittenden stone mansion; next the residence of Mr. James F. Clark; Mr. Henry,

John W. Allen, and J. C. Woolson. From the windows of our daguerrean rooms in the Merchants' Bank building, at the corner of Superior and Bank streets, we look over and across the street and see the old City Mills Store, Morgan and Root proprietors; next west, Smith & Dodd, shoe merchants; next Chas. P. Born, stoves, tinware, and plumbing; following next, the "Old City Buildings," occupied by cheap dealers in clothing, second-hand goods, etc., and the families of these thriftless or thrifty merchants, as you may choose, lived upstairs. In front, extending some six feet upon the sidewalk, was a platform eight or ten inches high, upon which to keep boxes and barrels for goods. The merchants with portions of their families occupied rickety chairs upon the platform, and in much-soiled shirt sleeves smoked their pipes while waiting for customers, thus mixing business with pleasure. The clapboards of the city buildings became warped and twisted from place. The broken windows were stuffed with rags or pasted over with paper. The structure was cause for anxiety by many citizens, and an earnest desire openly expressed was that fire would lap tongues of flame through its interior, and even caress the outer boundaries of its "gray and wrinkled front," but it would not. Evidently the structure bore a charmed life. It took no thought of cyclones, earthquakes, firebrands, or other calamities. There she stood, year after year, snapping her clapboard fingers at the winds, and possibly saying, "Come off," or "Bring on your bears — who's afraid!" Continuing west were Chris. Mullen, auctioneer; L. F. & S. Burgess, grocers; C. H. Robison, clothier; Seaman & Smith, boots and shoes; Hartness, Hill & Hay, bankers; Mygatt & Brown, bankers; Kelly's Hall; the Athenæum Theatre, where sang Jenny Lind, where played Anna Cora Mowatt, Julia Dean, Eliza Logan, and other bright stars of that period; next comes the *Cleveland Leader* building; the American House, Wm. Milford, proprietor. Continuing down the street: Gaylord & Hammond, druggists; N. Heisel, confectionery; Dr. McKenzie, druggist; Mrs. Keppler, cigars and snuff; Robt. Bailey, stoves and tinware; Mould & Numsen, confections and fruits; Powers' gun store; Gorham & Aplin, bakers; Geo. Williams, banker; Kennedy, DeForest & Randall, stoves and furnaces; Reynolds, hardware; the *Plain Dealer* printing establishment. On the corner opposite our studio was the Weddell House, the finest hotel in Cleveland at that time. Down the street toward the lake to Frankfort street was filled in with small buildings. On the corner of Frankfort and Bank streets was

F. Fleckenstein, Photographer, Faribault, Minn.

A MINNESOTA TROUT BROOK.

Wm. Bradford's place. Mr. Bradford was a conspicuous figure as a typical Englishman of the old school. He wore a florid countenance, knee breeches and shoe buckles. When on the street he was accompanied by a lot of dogs, and his " half and half " was undisputed. Just below his place down Bank street was the store of A. M. Beebe, dealer in Yankee notions; next were the express offices and the Johnson block, in which was the lodge of Knights of Malta, an honorable order, embracing in its membership many prominent citizens, among which the clergy was represented. They were distinguished for the extravagance in the regalia worn, and their ability to see the point of a joke. Some old members laugh to this day at mention of the funny happenings. A step down Centre street from Bank was the theatre, where in great style, for those days, the drama was presented to the *élite* of the city.

A few years later came " Foster's Varieties," on the east side of Bank street, near the Angier House. Quite a dream of beauty it was, and a pride to Clevelanders. Its name was changed to Academy of Music, as was also that of the " Angier House " to the Kennard, and by those names are still known. Looking down from our studio window into Bank street on a Saturday morning, there was always a stir of interesting activity to be seen. In front of O. Cutter's auction store the accumulation of household furniture would be moved out of the store onto the sidewalk for the usual Saturday sale. Mr. Cutter liked a crowd, and a good way to get it was to blockade the sidewalk. From a little distance a stranger would be led to think that a dog fight was in progress, while in fact merely Mr. Cutter and his son " Ed.," with sales book and cash box in hand, were making most of the noise. Citizen Sam. Baldwin was always on hand and generally was a liberal purchaser. Next to Cutter was the *Cleveland Herald* office, together with post-office and news depot, with funny Charley Backus as clerk. The interviews between Charles Backus and Mr. Irad Kelley were worth buying a reserved seat to hear. Charles could provoke Mr. Kelley to skin his teeth to a brighter glisten than any other citizen of Cleveland. Next was " Ki." Geer's livery stable, with broad plank plaza usually well furnished with a row of strong, splint-bottom arm-chairs, reaching within the entrance as well as out upon the sidewalk approach to the stable, presenting more the appearance of a popular club house than a home for carriages and horses. These chairs were occupied by various visitors, the list including, beside " Ki.": Benj. Harrington, Basil Spangler, Stoughton Bliss, Judge

Starkweather, James Pannell, George Morrill, Seymour Race, Dave Price, Crock Scovill, Jabe Fitch Fairbanks, Major Barker, James Barnett, Doct. Gordon, Dick Creighton and others. They enjoyed their cigars; exchanged fish stories, and when a leg was not thrown over the arm of a chair they were whittling at the foremost end of it. In this list the names of members of the Snollygoster Club of Camp Gilbert will be recognized by old citizens. Next to Geer's on the north was George Speed's

The Zwiefel Studio, Duluth, Minn.

CUPID.

place, a famous place of refreshment, well known to those "an hungered and athirst." Mrs. Speed, a cheery, helpful little body, looked after the wants and comforts of the customers most diligently. It would hardly have been "Speed's" without her. Louis Heiman, tailor, who could press trousers and take the bag out of the knees equal to any man in Cleveland, came next. On the corner of Frankfort and Bank lived Patrick Farley, a good Democrat and good citizen. He was very happy one morning because a son was born to him. Many friends were invited in to see the boy and congratulate the father. Stoughton Bliss was given the honor of writing the boy's name in the family Bible — John H. Farley — twice mayor of Cleveland; a man of backbone.

Taking another morning walk west on Superior street from the Weddell House as starting point, we go down looking into windows and reading signs as we pass. Here is Cowles & Albertson, jewelers; Aiken & Coon, also jewelers; Hancock & Pynchon, tailors; Sacketts, dry-goods. Next is the Franklin House, from which stage coaches for all points start out and to which they return; at this time there were no railways at Cleveland. Next is John Shelly, tailor; N. E. Crittenden, jeweler; Judd & Coffin, dry-goods; Whitman & Standard, bankers; Edward Clark, banker; N. Dockstader, hats; Worthington & Stair, hats; Brooks, crockery; Sanford & Hayward, printers and bookbinders; Rohrheimer, cigars; Geo. Worthington, hardware. On the corner of Superior and Water streets the sidewalk was garnished with great potash kettles, anchors and cables, and year after year they remained there lorn and rusty. I became well acquainted with them from seeing them so frequently, and wondered if any were ever sold. Crossing over to the other side of Superior, to return, we look down Superior street hill, and we see the New England Hotel, a really fine structure, and a well-kept hostelry; but built when the location was justified under the supposition that the hotel should be near the boat landing for lake passengers, and that Cleveland " under the hill " was to be the main point of business activity. One night this fine hotel was destroyed by fire, and it was no longer considered a good site for another to take its place. The former Atwater building stood with a much broader front across the foot of Superior street than its successor presents, as all that portion of the street representing viaduct approach was taken from the site of the original building. We now go through the lower portions of St. Clair, Water and Lake streets, and find it an aristocratic quarter. The solid men of the city; the representatives of wealth and fashion built their homes down-town and believed they had chosen the most desirable and most pleasant part of the city. The lake is always there; it is always grand in its vastness and beauty; a magnificent ocean animated in its expressions. Sometimes calm as a pane of glass; as innocent as a baby's smile; its beach of yielding sand inviting to the bare feet of children; the lap of its gentle ripples over the pebbles of the shore are welcome to the ear, and pleasant to the eye. A very gentle breeze ruffles the surface to slight agitations like musical whispers sweet to listen to. It sometimes takes on

C. M. Hayes Co., Photographers, Detroit, Mich.

PROF. A. H. GRIFFITH,

Director of Art Museum, Detroit, Mich.

The stranger coming to the city soon seeks her out. The old "light tower" on the hill, replaced by a better and taller one years ago; "Stockley's Pier," reaching out into deep water, are landmarks. Graybeards of today have caught fish from its oaken planks, and have dived from it into the refreshing deep. A few straggling piles, worn with the dash of waves and floating ice, still remain to hold the name. The "beauty spot" of Cleveland is from Lake street to the water's edge. That it was not taken for a public park years ago was one of the "mistakes of Moses," the city's founder. From the lake we walk across the business

a threat of warning — a phase acceptable to sailors, perhaps, but unwelcome to the timid. In the fierce moods of squall or storm, it becomes wild, dangerous, cruel. Viewed from the safe shore it is grand, something terrible to look upon; but to be in a tossing, plunging boat with a barely possible chance for landing, or of rescue, would be an experience to be remembered. The night may go boisterously to bed; the sun may find laughing dimples in the morning. Be she on a rampage or be she frolicsome in a glee, still there is our lake. Whether fair or wild she is interesting and people love to look upon her face.

Horton & Co., Photographers, Cleveland, O.

OUR GLADYS.

section through Water street and look upon the river toward
University Heights. Opening our eyes upon the valley lying
between what was the high banks on which, on one side, was
Ohio City, and on the other, Old Cleveland; the valley reaching
toward the heights, we see today, a city of mills, of forges, of
manufactories, of bridges, viaducts; the great lumber district,
stone yards, and great freight houses, and a rush of business activity incident to a prosperous city. But in the early fifties when I
took my morning walks, the river wound its crooked way through
a marshy valley. Beside it was the canal with its weigh-lock under
the Cleveland hill. Occasionally a boat moved its lazy way through
the canal; its motive power being a horse, possibly two, plodding
along the towpath, with the " engineer," a humped and sleepy-
looking boy, astride of one of the poky horses, making a typical
representation of commerce " as she were " in those days. Beyond
the river toward the opposite heights was a great space like a
prairie of marshy grass, known as Scranton's flats. Beside the
river bed, near where the Big Four tracks now run, was a brick
dwelling, the residence of Mr. Joel Scranton, the agent of the
extensive lands of the Connecticut Western Reserve Land Co., which
was controlled by Mr. Averill of Cooperstown, New York. That brick
dwelling was the only building on the flats. Later this tract of land
was purchased by Mr. Silas S. Stone, who foresaw a future value
for it, and soon these lands became known as " Stone's Pastures."
The growth of the city found a want of manufacturing and storage
space, and Stone's pastures were soon absorbed. The market district on Ontario street, south from the Public Square, was a busy
and interesting place. Market gardeners, butchers and hucksters
filled the streets, as well as the market house, three times a week.
On market days, when gardens gave fresh offerings, the products of
the dairy and the butcher shop were fresh and sweet, the good
housewife went forth to skirmish, to inspect, and to buy. Besides
filling the larder there was the pleasure of meeting neighbors and
friends, in having little impromptu visits, and in exchanging greet-
ings. Truly there is pleasure in marketing as well as attending
auctions which is dear to the woman's heart. Passing down Ontario street from market to the Square and turning east into Euclid
street, we find here, too, the residences of prominent citizens — that
of Richard F. Winslow, Edmund Clark, Dr. E. Cushing, E. Ster-
ling, Geo. F. Marshall, Philo Scovill, Benj. Harrington, and St.
Paul's Church, which was then on the corner of Euclid and Sheriff

streets, but long ago replaced by business houses.   Farther east on
Euclid was the Ursuline Convent, and Dr. Miles's residence, now
the Union Club house.   Back to the Square again, on the north side
of Euclid avenue, where now stands the sixteen-story Williamson
Building, was the then Delmonico's of Cleveland — "Stacy's."   Oh!
the ice creams! which from spoon to mouth carried a streak of
pleasure down happy necks, at the tête-à-tête tables in that blissful
establishment, with genial " Josiah " beaming upon happy customers.   And the dancing hall upstairs, where, upon masquerade
occasions, might be seen members of the royal families (known by
their costumes), sitting in dignified silence, while happy voices and
laughter were heard in the " banquet hall " opposite.   Poor chaps!
their last shilling had been paid for their costumes, and the price
of a supper was not in their clothes; but such is life!   We may
point with pride to the Williamson Building, which if fifty stories
high could not blot out the delightful remembrances of " Stacy's; "
just the mention of his name to this day leaves an ice-creamy taste
in the mouths of thousands.   From Stacy's east were residences
of Samuel Williamson, Dr. Strickland, L. Benedict, H. Nottingham,
Geo. A. Benedict, Henry Chisholm, M. B. Scott, H. F. Gaylord,
Lemuel Crawford, W. S. C. Otis, and the Plymouth Church.

J. B. Hoff, Photographer, Delphos, O.

LITTLE BESS.

CHAPTER XIX.

SUNSETS.

In the late afternoons of spring and summer, after hours of business, I found it pleasant to drift about making acquaintance with new localities and revisiting the more attractive ones. I found that so pleasant and interesting a place as Cleveland was constantly presenting new material in this way. The especial point of interest was the lake front, and in that direction people by hundreds sauntered of an evening to behold the grandeur of the sunsets. Along the banks sloping to the lake from a height of fifty feet to the water, a patient, admiring crowd would gather daily, and particularly on evenings following a storm or shower of rain; when on "clearing up" the atmosphere was purified by the wash from the clouds, a fresher, brighter glory of color would appear in the western sky and be reflected throughout the firmament. Old Sol comes along on his daily trudge, sending his warmth and light to us all —never forgetting even a blade of grass, nor the broad fields whence comes our daily bread. He even takes a squint at us mites on the bank and throws our shadows over the grass. We squint back at him; we squint and we blink at his wondrous light, whose brilliancy is dazzling. We watch him as nearer he slowly drops to the sea of Lake Erie, into whose waters he finally appears to sink. We forget, because we cannot see that the land of Canada is just beyond. As lower and lower he sinks, the brilliancy of color increases and broadens; colors and tints of delicacy undreamed of; ever unseen, except in his domain. As he dips the lower rim of his circle behind the horizon he throws a path of gold upon the shimmering surface of the water which appears as an illuminated highway for heavenly chariots leading to the great beyond. Through openings of the gorgeous curtain of sun coloring, glimpses of another world could easily be imagined as seen through portals of divine grandeur where the gates of pearl are studded with jewels and hinged upon gold. This grandeur, painted by the brush of Omnipotence and spread over the heavens, is God's promise to the world. It is "hung upon the line" and for free exhibition to the

The Baker Art Studio, Photographers, Columbus, O.

THE BRIDE.

least as well as to the greatest of earth.   Canvases from masters of
the past, and the present, may glow in paint after an earthly fashion, but they pale and sicken in comparison with the work of the
divine Master whose clouds they can never imitate.

As good " Sol " drops out of sight, under a coverlet of water,
he tips us a wink, as if to say, " Good-night!   I'll be around again
in the morning."   Steamers coming home; steamers starting out
for other ports; sailboats with canvas wide out, slowly making their
journeys, burdened heavily, minding the winds which were pushing
them along their patient way; fishing boats gently tossed and
nodding in the foreground; row boats gliding smoothly over the
water, all made pleasant accessories to the picture.

The front seats to this exhibition were a lot of large building
stone scattered about upon the grass at the brow of the bank, and
each evening a few more were found which had been brought
during the day.   The meaning of this was not understood by some
of the visitors, and I remember asking what was to be done with
the stone, and was told the United States government was commencing to build a hospital for sick and disabled sailors to be called
" Marine Hospital."   We all thought it a commendable thing for
Uncle Sam to do, and gave it hearty approval.   From that time on
we severally kept a careful watch over the enterprise and became,
in a way, inspectors of stone.   I confess I admired the quality of
the blocks which were heavy, clean, and of good gray shade.   Some
of my fellow inspectors, more critical than others, found it necessary to feel the surface of those good stones by passing their hands
carefully over them in gentle caresses, and if a suggestion of chip
or scale was found they would test it with the thumb nail.

I was not so searchingly particular, but was content that the
stones made a good temporary seat, and was satisfied that we
would have a good job, being willing to trust Uncle Sam.   I had
not become a taxpayer at that time, and was not inclined to watch
details.   I kept up my attendance regularly and faithfully, much
enjoying the phases of cloud effect and color over the lake, and
when those good stone blocks had been properly placed, and a fine
hospital finished, I sought other seats.   When in the march of
progress our growing commercial city dropped her swaddling
clothes and took on wraps of different " cloud effects," made up of
floating pellets of soot, or bituminous smudge of unconsumed fuel
which had a habit of floating off over our beautiful lake and forming a wall of darkness, shutting out from us the glory of sunsets,

THE DANCING GIRL.

I lost the habit of visiting the old haunts. The stones which were then clean and inviting are now blackened walls and no longer attractive. I had a liking for boats, and for sailor men. I visited the vessels in port, and enjoyed talking with the big-hearted and open-fisted fellows. I had a brother who had " plowed the briny " after whales. An old shipmate of his sailed a vessel in the upper lakes trade, running into Cleveland twice a month. I knew nothing of this until by accident I met him on board his big schooner. He discovered in me the likeness to my brother and, asking my name, in three minutes we were as old friends. He was Jack Lucas, from New Bedford, who had been my brother's close friend; who had brought to my mother her son's last message; who stood beside his grave as his body was given back to earth in a far-off island of the sea. My pleasure at meeting Captain Lucas was equalled by his pleasure in meeting me. I took Sunday dinner with him on board; we had " duff," a dish peculiar to the mariner; it was a bit solid, but very palatable. He opened a bottle of wine, which made a pleasant wash for it, and paved the way to a fine appreciation of our pipes. From out of his chest he brought forth to show me a number of curious and ingenious things made by sailors in their idle hours at sea, when becalmed, or to help to wear through a dull watch. The teeth of whales and of the walrus, engraved and carved as ornaments, were among them and some of which gave evidence of skill. He showed me a pipe-bowl carved from a walrus tusk by an old English tar which was quite wonderful as a piece of amateur work. The bowl was a basket held upon the shoulders of a typical shore woman of Brittany. The strong face of the hardy people of whom she was a type was faithfully given; her arms raised to grasp the edge of the basket as the bottom rested upon or between the shoulders; the expression suggesting a heavy load. The weaving

of the splints forming the body of the basket, passing over and
under, was very natural. It was quite a work of art, and I felt
sure the maker had not passed all his life hunting whales. The
captain put forth every effort to entertain me; invited me to make
a trip up the lakes with him, which I gratefully accepted. The
pleasant hours of that trip will never be forgotten. The moon was
never more friendly; never showed a brighter face than on the
nights when Captain Lucas and myself lay wondering and watching
her from our impromptu couches of coiled rope and canvas, on the
deck. The lazy swing of the vessel's sails, with an occasional lurch
of her masts and a creak of overstrained block, and the wash of the
water against the body of the good *Mary Jane*, made lullaby for a
tired sailor, or pleasant accompaniment for forecastle yarns by a
good spinner. There are doubtless as equally gifted story-tellers
as he, also those who can handle adjectives of a salty flavor, inter-
spersed with "emphasizers" known to the sailor man, as easily as
he, but Captain Jack Lucas, while not a graduate of a forecastle
university of nautical lore, was a most entertaining man. He possessed the happy faculty of making his listener *see* the situation.
That my lost brother cut a figure in some of these tales of the
trackless sea, gave them added interest to me. If it were a prize
contest for supremacy in the matter of concentrated salt romance,
I would back my friend Captain Jack Lucas against Dr. Depew. I
enjoyed the odor of tar in the rigging. I liked the smell of marline
and oakum; and fancied a sort of sentiment in it. The phrase
"tarred with a stick," as indicating character or disposition in
people, is sometimes quite apt. It sets the mind at work; if followed up, it intuitively leads — where? The human family is more
or less touched with it. The variety of stick and quality of tar
takes wide range. There are sticks crooked and coarse; tar that is
black, sticky and rank of odor; the man tainted with such an
extreme sample is not quite fortunate; persons of clean character,
pure thoughts and sensitive impressions shudder at proximity to
such; a dog instinctively growls and shows his teeth at approach
of a person so tarred. Another stick, smooth of grain; a tar more
diluted, strained through Christian grace and mixed with the milk of
human kindness, is as a blessing from God. With such were our
innocent sisters and blessed mothers tipped. I like to fancy a great
urn filled with refined and distilled tar diluted with honey, balms,
and sweet perfumes, as standing at the threshold of life, where unseen angels dip the tips of their wings and anoint the incoming babes.

CHAPTER XX.

THE SWEET SINGER OF MICHIGAN.

"THE SWEET SINGER OF MICHIGAN."

One of the most interesting and unique experiences of my life came as a kind of diversion in the rather prosaic life of the photographer, and that was my dive, as I may say, into the mystic realms of poesy and song alonger Mrs. Julia A. Moore, " The Sweet Singer of Michigan." One of her literary fragments in falling into my hands struck my " funny bone " with such "a resounding crash" that I could not, by the most laborious effort, secure the bodily rest usually regarded as requisite to the human frame, until I had communicated with the feminine bard of the lumber regions of the northwest. I secured the front seat of the show when her poems " came down the pike " one by one, at my solicitation, until I had collected quite a number, and I must confess that they burned in my pockets like a boy's first " fip'ny bit," until I was compelled to mature a plan by which these effusions of the Muse could be given to the public. It is a well-known fact among critics that two kinds of poetry, and only two, go in the public estimation and are worth anything in the market. One kind is the very good and the other is the very bad. Mediocre poetry is a drug in the marts, valueless in a commercial sense. Believing that a thinking, discriminating public could be trusted with the verdict in the case, I arranged for the publication of the poems in a copyrighted book. I recall now, that the poetess in the strain of production in several of her poems approached the mediocre in her work, and then I would have to write her that she was pondering over her work too much, and that I could not use her productions. I would urge her to dash off her poems, just as Byron and all the great geniuses, presumably, had done, and after these gentle chidings the Muse would seek the old channels. There was an introductory preface desired for the book, and " The Sweet Singer " promptly furnished the following:

DEAR FRIENDS:

This book is composed of truthful pieces. All those which speak of being killed, died, or drowned are truthful songs. Others are more truth than poetry. They are all composed by the Author.

I was born in Plainfield, and lived there until I was ten years of age. Then my parents removed to Algoma, where they have lived until the present day, and I live near them one mile west of Edgerton.

JULIA A. MOORE.

The launching of the book was accompanied by the following circular:

CLEVELAND, O., October, 1877.

DEAR SIR:

Having been honored by the gifted lady of Michigan in being entrusted with the publication of her poems, I give myself the pleasure of handing you herewith a copy of the same, with my respectful compliments.

It will prove a health lift to the overtaxed brain; it *may* divert the despondent from suicide. It should enable the reader to forget the " stringency," and guide the thoughts into pleasanter channels. It opens a new lead in literature, and is sure to carry conviction. It *must* be productive of good to humanity. If you have the good of your fellow creatures at heart, and would contribute your mite towards putting them in the way of finding this little volume, the thanks of a grateful people (including authoress and publisher) would be yours. If a sufficient success should attend the sale of this work, it is our purpose to complete the Washington Monument.

Very truly yours,
J. F. RYDER,
239 Superior Street.

I sent copies of the book to all the leading newspapers and famous writers of the day, and the reviews and comments on the unique publication made an epoch of the time in the literary world, splitting the globe, as it were, with a broad smile, from New York to the Golden Gate. Such papers as the New York *Tribune, Herald, Sun ;* the Boston *Globe,* Chicago *Tribune,* Louisville *Courier-Journal,* and others seemed to vie with each other in getting spicy interviews with the new star in the literary firmament. Bill Nye

LITTLE SWEETHEART.

devoted some four columns of the Denver *Tribune* to the glorifica-
tion of the Michigan poetess, as follows:

[Correspondence of *The Tribune.*]

Through the courtesy of a popular young lady of Chicago, who
recognizes struggling genius at all times, I have been permitted to
carefully read and enjoy the lays of "The Sweet Singer of Michigan," and I ask the readers of *The Tribune* to come with me a few
moments into the great field of literature, while we flit from flower
to flower on the wings of the Muse. There are few, indeed, of us
who do not love the heaven-born music of true poesy. Hardened,
indeed, must he be whose soul is dead to the glad song of the true
poet, and we can but pity the gross, brutal nature which refuses to
throb and burn with spiritual fire lighted with coals from the altar
of the gods. I speak only for myself when I say that seven or
eight twangs of the lyre stir my impressible nature so that I rise
above the cares and woes of this earthly life, and I paw the ground
and yearn for the unyearnable, and howl. Julia A. Moore, better
known as "The Sweet Singer of Michigan," was born some time
previous to the opening of this chapter, of poor but honest parents;
and although she couldn't have custard pie and frosted cake every
day, she was happy, as appears by a little poem in the collection
entitled, "The Author's Early Life," in which she says:

> My heart was gay and happy,
>   This was ever in my mind,
> There is better days a-coming,
>   And I hope some day to find
> Myself capable of composing.
>   It was my heart's delight
> To compose on a sentimental subject
>   If it came in my mind just right.

This would show that the Muse was getting in its work, as I
might say, even while yet Julia was a little nut-brown maid trudg-
ing along to school with bare feet that looked like the back of a
warty toad. In my visions I see her now standing in front of the
teacher's desk, soaking the first three joints of her thumb in her
rosebud mouth and trying to work her off toe into a knot-hole in the
floor, while outside, the turtle dove and the masculine Michigan
mule softly coo to their mates. A portrait of the author appears
on the cover of the little volume. It is a very striking face. There
are lines of care about the mouth — that is, part way around the

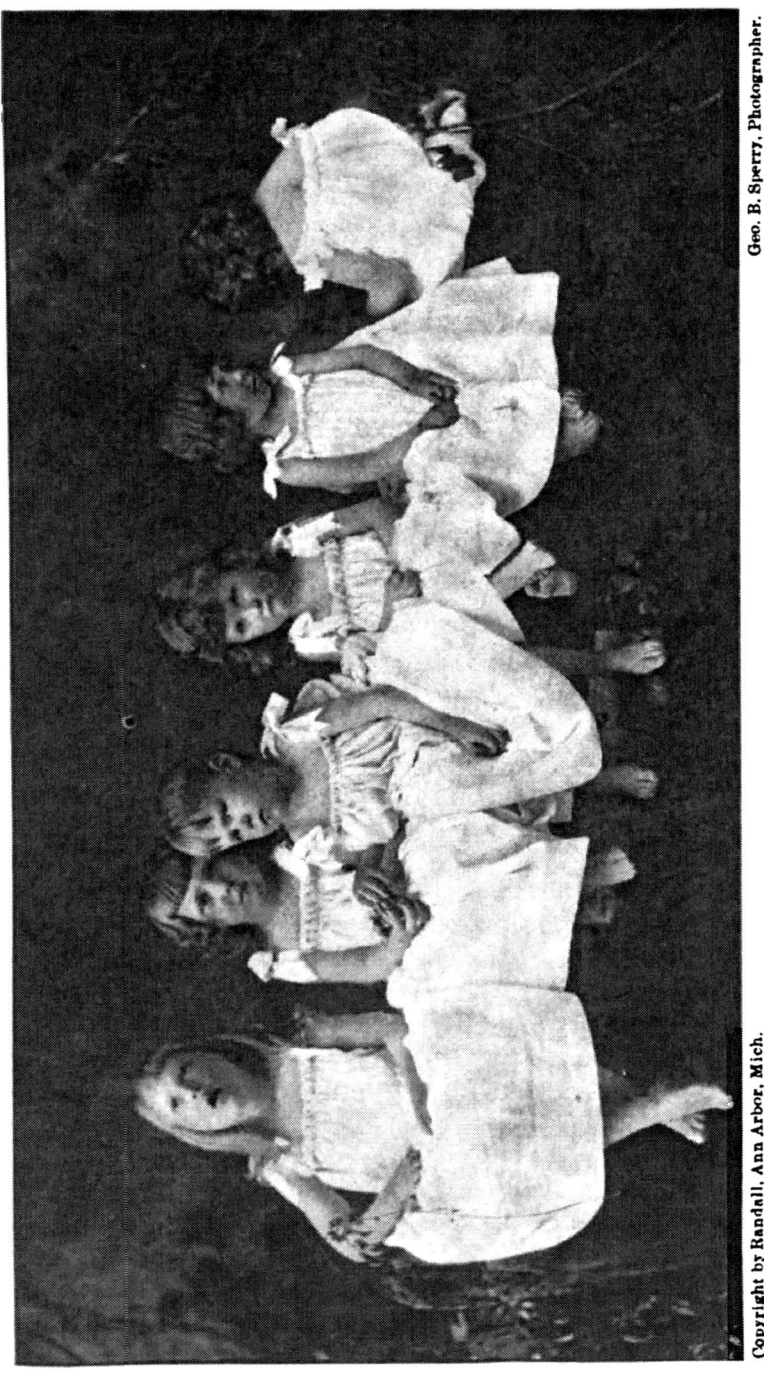

Geo. B. Sperry, Photographer.

Copyright by Randall, Ann Arbor, Mich.

mouth. They did not reach all the way around because they didn't have time. Lines of care are willing to do anything that is reasonable, but they can't reach around the North Park without getting fatigued. These lines of care and pain look to the student of physiognomy as though the author had lost a good deal of sleep trying to compose obituary poems. The brow is slightly drawn, too, as though her corns might be hurting her. Julia wears her hair plain, like Alfred Tennyson and Sitting Bull. It hangs down her back in perfect abandon and wild profusion, shedding bear's oil over the collar of her delaine dress, regardless of expense.

I can not illustrate or describe the early vision of dimpled loveliness which Julia presented in her childhood better than by giving a little gem from " My Infant Days: "

> When I was a little infant,
>   And I lay in mother's arms,
> Then I felt the gentle pressure
>   Of a loving mother's arms.
>
> " Go to sleep my little baby,
>   Go to sleep," mamma would say;
> " O, will not my little baby
>   Go to sleep for ma to-day?"

When I read this little thing the other day it broke me all up. It took me back to my childhood days when I lay in my little trundle bed, and was wakeful and had a raging thirst insomuch that I used to want a drink of water every fifteen seconds. Mamma didn't ask if I would " go to sleep for ma, today." She used to turn the bedclothes back over the footboard so that she could have plenty of sea room, and then she would take an old sewing machine belt and it would sigh through the agitated air for a few moments pretty plenty, till the writer of these lines would conclude to sob himself to sleep, and anon through the night he would dream that he had backed up against the Hill Smelting Works. That's the kind of " Go to sleep for ma today " that comes up vividly to my mind.

But I must give another stanza or two from Julia's collection — as showing how this gifted writer can, with a word, dispel the chilling temperature of December and run the thermometer up to 100 degrees in the shade. I will quote from the death of " Little Henry: "

MR. HUBBELL, OF ROCHESTER, N. Y., ON A TRIP OUT WEST, TAKES HIS
KODAK WITH HIM.

It was on the eleventh of December,
  On a cold and windy day,
Just at the close of evening
  When the sunlight fades away,
Little Henry he was dying,
  In his little crib he lay,
With the soft winds around him sighing,
  From early morn till close of day.

One of Julia's poems opens out in such a cheerful, pleasant
way that I wish I could give it all, but space forbids. She tunes
her lyre so that it will mash all right and then says:

Come all, kind friends, both far and near,
O come, and see what you can hear.

Then she proceeds to slaughter some one. In looking over her
poems one is struck with the terrible mortality which they show.
Julia is worse than a Gatling gun. I have counted twenty-one
killed and nine wounded in the small volume which she has given
to the public. In giving the circumstances which attended the
death of one of her subjects, and the economical principles of the
deceased, she says:

And he was sick and very bad,
  Poor boy, he thought, no doubt,
If he came home in a smoking car
  His money would hold out.
He started to come back alone,
  He came one-third the way.
One evening, in the car alone,
  His spirit fled away.

That's the way Julia kills off a young man just as we get interested in him.   You just begin to like one of her heroes or heroines and Julia proceeds to lay said hero or heroine out colder than a wedge.   A sad, sad thing, which goes to the tune of Belle Mahone, starts out as follows:

> " Once there lived a lady fair,
>   With black eyes and curly hair;
>   She has left this world of care
>   Sweet Carrie Monroe."

To which I have added, in my poor weak way —

> She could not her sorrows bear,
> For she was a dumpling rare;
> She has clum the golden stair,
>   Sweet Carrie Monroe.

> 'Twas indeed a day of gloom
> When we gathered in her room,
> While she cantered up the flume,
>   Sweet Carrie Monroe.

I will give but one more example of Julia's exquisite word-painting, and then after a word or two relative to her style generally I will close.

After speaking tearfully of her life as a child, she says:

> My childhood days have passed and gone,
>   And it fills my heart with pain
> To think that youth will never more
>   Return to me again.
> And now, kind friends, what I have wrote
>   I hope you will pass o'er,
> And not criticise, as some have done,
>   Hitherto herebefore.

I know that it ill becomes me to assume the prerogative of criticising a poet's style or even to suggest any improvements, but sometimes an outsider may be able to stand off, as it were, and see little defects in a masterpiece which the author can not see.   One suggestion will, I know, be accepted as coming from one who never says anything but in the kindest spirit.   I think that Julia takes advantage of her poetic license.   A poetic license, as I understand it, simply allows the poet to jump the 15 over the 14 in order to bring in the proper rhyme, but it does not allow the writer to usurp the management of the entire system of worlds, and introduce dog-days and ice-cream between Christmas and New Year.

P. S. Ryder, Photographer, Syracuse, N. Y.

WAITING.

It does not in any way allow the contractor of prize funeral puffs
to sandwich a tropical evening, with the scent of orange blossom
and mignonette, in between two December days in Michigan that
would freeze the lightning-rods off the houses; when the owners
of cast-iron dogs have to bring them in and stand them behind the
parlor stove. Julia can't fool me much on Michigan winters.
When the seductive breath from the north comes soughing across
Lake Superior, redolent with the blossom rock of the copper mines
and dead cranberry vines and slippery-elm bark, the poet or poetess
who could maliciously crawl into a buffalo overcoat and write a
dirge that worked in " sighing soft winds," just for the benefit of
one whose spirit is in a land where house plants never freeze,
should have no poetic license.

We have too many poets in our glorious republic who ought to
be peeling the epidermis off a bull train; and too many poetesses
who would succeed better boiling soap-grease or spiking a 6 x 8
patch on the quarter-deck of a faithful husband's overalls. I do
not refer entirely to Julia in the last few lines, for Julia is not
deserving of such criticism. She was never intended to do the
drudgery of housework. She is too frail. She couldn't cook,
because her cake would be sad and her soft, wavy hair, like the
mane of Cayuse plug, would get in the codfish balls and cling to
the butter. No, Julia, you don't look like a woman whose career
as a housewife would be a success. From the mournful look in
your limpid eye, I would say that your lignum-vitæ bread and cel-
luloid custard pie, and indestructible waffles, and fire-proof pancakes,
and burglar-proof chicken-pie would give you away. Your mind
would be far away in the poet's realm, and you would put shoe-
blacking in the blanc mange, and silver gloss starch in the tea, and
cod liver oil in the sponge cake. So, Julia, you may continue right
along as you are doing. It don't do much harm, and no doubt it
does you a heap of good.

                                                    BILL NYE.

In acknowledgment of the receipt of the book of poems which
had been sent to a carefully selected list of publications and newspapers, the current literature of the times was fairly stormed by
the literary critics who made the fair, stout singer and her muse a
target for literary mud balls. In commenting upon the furor of the
time, the poetess says: " Some of the editors that has spoken in a
scandalous manner have went beyond reason."

There was scarcely a newspaper of any prominence that did

not, in some manner, exploit the "sweet singer," and from an old scrap-book made of the clippings at the time, the following are scissored:

[New York *World.*]

Mrs. Julia A. Moore's verses may be rough, but so were the "bars" that unquestionably prowled around her cradle even as the honeyed bees about that of the Grecian bard. For, as she expressly says:

In the days of my early childhood,
 Kent County was quite wild,
Especially the towns I lived in
 When I was a little child.

The sweet singer of Michigan, while yet a child nor yet a fool to fame, seems to have lisped in numbers, for she says she found herself

. . . capable of composing.
 It was my heart's delight
To compose on a sentimental subject;
 If it came in my mind just right.

Notwithstanding this truly admirable confession of literary faith, which, as the reader will see, precludes any perfunctory poetizing, the writer has that nervous dread of criticism attributed to more than one of her fellow poets, for she expressly says that she hopes her readers will

Not criticise, as some have done
 Hitherto, herebefore.

P. S. Ryder, Photographer, Syracuse, N. Y.

MARGUERITE.

Nevertheless, notwithstanding, it is the privilege of those who, in Disraeli's phrase, would fail to write such verses as Mrs. Moore's to shy at her, as she sings in the back-yard of the emotions, the boot-jacks of criticism.   It is not even sure that the fact that in a poem on the Centennial she makes " nation " rhyme to " waving " — as the Irishman played the fiddle neither by note nor by ear, but by main strength — will appease the wrath of the miserable carpers by whom " The Baroness of New York " is regarded as scarcely superior to " Aurora Leigh " or " The Princess."   In justice — to ourselves — we must give the chorus:

> Centennial! Centennial!
>   Hurrah to the Centennial;
> And many, many people gone
>   To our national Centennial.

So excellent a burden to a song has not exasperated us since we first heard wailed in the classic precincts of M. Todgers's Commercial Boarding-House that immortal air:

> So, hail to the vessel of Pecksniff, the sire,
>   And favoring breezes to fan,
> While mermaids float round it and proudly admire
>   The architect, father and man.

The genius of Mrs. Julia A. Moore, as Shaw says of John Webster, is essentially gloomy.   We stumble over graves and run against monuments, and welter in obituary notices, and here in her verse are all trappings forbid, save the tinsel that shone in the dark coffin lid.   Frinstance, we begin with the poem of " John Robinson," set to the familiar air of " The Drunkard:"

> His father and mother being dead,
> It left him an orphan boy.
> Kind friends they thought 'twould do him good
> To travel for his health;
> To California he did go
> With his Uncle Zera French.

Unhappily, " poor Jonny " died on his road back (in a smoking-car), an incident which, as it inspired the poem from which the lines above are taken, we cannot too keenly regret.   Hardly, however, can we say " Jack Robinson!" than we are confronted with the elegy of " The Brave Page Boys," which (as sung to the familiar air of " The Fierce Discharge ") lends new terror to social assemblies in Kent Co., Mich.:

From painting by A. M. Willard, Cleveland, O.

PITCHING THE TUNE.

Fernando Page the second son,
    Served in the Infantriege,
He was wounded — lost both his feet,
    On duty at Yorktown siege.
Charles F. Page was a noble son,
    In '64 did enless
And in the same year he was killed
    In the fight of the Wilderness.

It will be observed that we have trimmed Mrs. Moore's rhyth-
mic ear to make it more symmetrical to the reader's eye.   The fate
of the two brave Page boys, already enumerated, was mild compared with that of their younger brother Enos:

In Eight Michigan Cavalry
    This boy he did enlist;
His life was almost despaired of,
    On account of numerous fits,
Caused by drinking water poisoned —
    Effects cannot outgrow;
In northern Alabama, I hear,
    There came this dreadful blow.

Would that this page contained not only seven columns, but seventy times seven; then might we do justice to Hiram Helsel (the charnel air of this dirge is " Three Grains of Corn "):

> He was a small boy of his age;
> When he was five years or so
> Was shocked by lightning while to play,
> And it caused him not to grow.

Then, also, might we prepare to shed a sufficiency of tears over William Upson, whose elegy, after showing what a consolation it was to his mother to have his remains brought home from Nashville, proceeds to dash the consoling cup from the lips of Mrs. Deacon Jesse Upson, as follows:

> She knows not that it was her son,
> His coffin could not be opened —
> It might be some one in his place
> For she could not see his noble face.
>
> He enrolled in eighteen sixty-three,
> The next day after Christmas eve;
> He died in eighteen sixty-four,
> Twenty-third of March, as I was told.

For a moment Mrs. Moore reverts to her own youth, when of her parents she was the eldest born. And they always called her Julia, in a mild and loving form, when, as she very neatly observes:

> My parents were poor and they could not dress me so,
> For they had not got the money to spare,
> And it may be better so, for I do not think fine clothes
> Make a person any better than they are.
>
> Remember never to judge people by their clothes,
> For our brave, noble Washington said,
> " Honorable are rags if a true heart they inclose,"
> And I found it was the truth when I married.

But the lapse is only for a moment, for on the next page Mrs. Moore returns to her themes, if not of damnation, at least of the dead. " Dearest Minnie, she has left us." It is the right hearse-driver's rank to market. The epithalamium of Lois House (air, " Sophronia's Farewell ") follows, to be succeeded by a scarcely less mournful lay of the seventeen months' suffering of " The Brave Volunteer: "

Chyler Davis,	This brave and noble volunteer,
He hailed from Oakfield town,	He left his home and friends,
He enlisted in the service,	For he dearly loved his country,
His native land to shield.	He went from Michigan.

Mrs. Moore's rhymes, so to speak, are based upon a bi-metallic standard to the " finer harmonies " of which, to quote from Long-fellow, we Eastern bondholders (whom she scourges in a poem that would inevitably destroy them from off the face of the earth with tetanus should they attempt to sing it — air, " We'll Rally Round the Flag ") are perhaps not awake.   But there is something grandly consistent in her system.   " Town " and " shield " rhyme indifferent well, but that is atoned for by this quotation from " Little Andrew: "

> On one bright and pleasant morning
>   His uncle thought it would be nice
> To take his dear little nephew
>   Down to play upon — a raft.

At the conclusion of this stanza we can almost see the " Sweet Singer of Michigan " disappearing around a sheltering crag of Parnassus, her tuneful thumb applied to her melodious nose, glee-fully exclaiming to the baffled reader, " You thought it would be — ' on the ice.'   Fooled again! "

We do not clearly see that we can afford to lay out the corpse of " Little Henry " in the circumscribed limits of this review, even though he inspired Mrs. Moore to risk dislocation of the roots of her tongue in rhyming " coals " with " curled."   We do not know, however, of anything in the range of contemporary obituary litera-ture to compare with the chorus:

> God has took their little treasure,
>   And his name I'll tell you now;
> He has gone from earth forever,
>   Their little Charles Henry House.

No, we know of nothing like this in modern or ancient litera-ture, not excepting the fiery, untamed psalms of Sternhold and Hopkins, or the verses of Nat Lee; and, upon the whole, we are not sorry.

In reading the poetry of Mrs. Moore, the reader often barks his tongue over the tombstones of members of the House family:

> They once did live at Edgerton,   It was William House's family,
> They once did live at Muskegon;   As fine a family as you see —
> From there they went to Chicago,   His family was eleven in all;
> Which proved their fatal overthrow.   I do not think it was very small.

(The poet, we think, does not sufficiently take into considera-tion the number of elegies, funerals, inquests, etc., that the House family had coldly to furnish forth.)

> The small-pox then was raging there,
> And oh it would not their house spare,
> For all but one was sick of them,
> A dreadful house it must have been.

The father died in the sure and certain hope that he would be embalmed, or at least laid out, in Mrs. Moore's book, and the care of providing for and burying the family devolved on his second son:

> Charles helped the sexton, I am told,
> To lay his form in the coffin cold —
> How sad, how sad, poor soul was he,
> When last his father's form did see.

> Minnie May House she had to go,
> And leave her friends that loved her so —
> She was a girl just in her teens,
> A lovely flower as e'er was seen.

> Minnie and her mother lay on one bed,
> And when Charles said, " Our Minnie is dead,'
> His mother then she did grow wild,
> And early after knew her child.

> They buried Minnie by her father's side,
> And left them there where they had died —
> Charles took his mother and brothers then
> And brought them back to Michigan.

> For the mother and the baby too
> Kind friends did all that they could do,
> But those poor souls they could not save,
> For now they're sleeping in their grave.

> Oh! what a noble son was he,
> His age was then only sixteen —
> Charles House's name I have told before,
> God bless his soul forever more.

It is gratifying to be able to close this review with an assurance that the vermifuge of the living present has been able to expel from the poetical system of the " Sweet Singer of Michigan " the worms of the tomb. Contrasted with her hearse-like airs is a comparatively joyous carol concerning the Grand Rapids Cricket Club, of which she says:

> Grand Rapids club that cricket play
>   Will soon be known afar —
> Much prouder do the members stand,
>   Like many a noble star.

Evan D. Evans, Photographer, Ithaca, N. Y.

A FAIR LADY.

In this poem several distinguished players are mentioned by name, though (such is the morbid impulse of Mrs. Moore, whose Pegasus is never happy except between the shafts of a hearse) these only obtain their distinction because of almost fatal accidents they have met with.   Frinstance, she says:

> And Mr. Follet is very brave,
>   A lighter player than the rest,
> He got struck severe at the fair ground,
>   For which *he took a rest*.

This we will now proceed to do — and we invite Mrs. Moore to do likewise.

[Cincinnati *Saturday Night*.]

The sad story of John Robinson is told in a song of the " Come, listen friends " order.   John was an orphan boy, but sickness overtaking him,

> " Kind friends they thought 'twould do him good
>   To travel for his health;
>   To California he did go
>   With his Uncle Zera French."

Captious critics might complain that French doesn't rhyme with health, but that was Uncle Zera's fault.   He might have had a name that *would* rhyme with health.   What are uncles for?   But " Jonny " gets homesick and writes a letter:

> It said, " Dear Brother, will you please
> Some money to me send,
> For I fear I have not got enough
> To bring me back again."

The brother takes some money and starts for California to bring him back, but too late.   John Robinson is already on his way:

> For he was sick, and very bad —
>   Poor boy, he thought, no doubt,
> If he came home in a smoking car
>   His money would hold out.
> He started to come back alone —
>   He came one-third the way —
> One evening in the car alone
>   His spirit fled away.

[Worcester (Mass.) *Daily Press*.]

There is, among the many gems composing her little book, one poem which will so saturate with tenderness the heart of the most hardened critic that he will lay aside his pen and involuntarily reach for his wipe. It treats of the hard luck of little Hiram Helsel, who

> Was shocked by lightning while out to play;
> It caused him not to grow.

He was five years of age when he was thus caused not to grow. In addition to this setback,

> His parents parted when he was small,
> And both are married again.
> How sad it was for them to meet
> And view his last remains.

Several stanzas later he dies and finds protection from a cruel father and an unnatural mother, likewise from the woes inflicted by his father's wife and his mother's husband, in that haven where

> . . . Grief and woes ne'er enters.

The dazzling success of the book carried us irresistibly into the lecture field; the first plunge was announced by the following, in the Cleveland *Leader :*

" The ' Sweet Singer of Michigan ' has been interviewed by a reporter of the *Inter-Ocean,* to whom she opens her honest heart. A portion of the conversation runs as follows:

" You must make considerable money from the sale of your books? "

" No, I don't make very much. Ryder (the publisher) makes the money. The most I make is what I sell myself. I have sold pretty near $29 worth of the books to the neighbors around here to send to their friends. As soon as I can go through the country reading my poems I think I can sell more of the books."

" Then you are going on the stage again? "

"'Yes, in March. I shall read in Cleveland one or two nights. Ryder offers me $100 a night and me and my old man's expenses. I have two gentlemen in Grand Rapids who want the refusal of all the other cities."

But in the interim I noticed that, as the days passed before we could get all things ready, the poetess began to express doubt regarding the public readings. This feeling appeared to grow upon her, until I became somewhat anxious, and sought by strategic chiding to rouse her drooping spirits; to give back-bone, as I thought, to " halting genius," but to no avail, until finally the meat axe fell, so to speak, when she wrote me to the effect that the shadow of the conventional stork had fallen once again athwart the domestic hearth, and she feared that people might make remarks, and she begged to be excused, which was speedily granted, and the " Sweet Singer " was given over to sweet domesticity.

CHAPTER XXI.

ARTEMUS WARD.

On going into the *Plain Dealer* editorial rooms one morning, I saw a new man and was introduced to him by head bookkeeper, Chas. E. Wilson, as Mr. Browne.   He was young, cheerful in manner; tall and slender; not quite up to date in style of dress, yet by no means shabby.   His hair was flaxen and very straight; his nose, the prominent feature of his face, was Romanesque — quite violently so, with a leaning to the left.   His eyes were blue gray with a twinkle in them; his mouth seemed so given to a merry laugh, so much in motion, that it was difficult to describe, so we let it pass.   It seemed as though bubbling in him was a lot of happiness which he made no effort to conceal, or hold back.   When we were introduced he was sitting at his table writing; he gave his leg a smart slap, arose and shook hands with me, and said he was glad to meet me.   I believed him, for he looked glad all the time.   You couldn't look at him but that he would laugh.   He laughed as he sat at his table writing, and when he had written a thing which pleased him he would slap his leg and laugh.   I noticed that George Hoyt and James Brokenshire who were sitting at their tables were pleased with his merriment, and were indulging in broad smiles.   As I bade him, with the others, "good morning," he said: "Come again, Me Liege."   I thanked him, said I would, and went my way thinking what a funny fellow he was.   Within a month thereafter there appeared in the columns of the *Plain Dealer* a funny letter signed "Artemus Ward."   The letter was an announcement that he, Artemus Ward, was in the show business; had a trained kangaroo, "a most amoosin' little cuss"; also some "snaix," and a collection of wax figures, which he called "a great moral show."   As he was coming to Cleveland to exhibit he made a proposition to the proprietor of the paper, that they "scratch each other's backs"—the publisher to write the show up vigorously, and the showman would have his handbills printed at his office, and give him free tickets for all his family. So I found my young friend of the gurgle and hay-colored hair to

Yourn till Deth,
Artemus Ward.

be the embryo humorist, just budded, and bursting into bloom. "Artemus," as from that time he was best known, soon had a city full of friends, myself and family among them. He sat at our table every Sunday; we learned to know him well and to enjoy his cheerful peculiarities. His humor was like a bubbling spring, always " on tap; " a merry laugh was always ready and easily called out. In his jaunts about town in quest of items — he was city editor — he often called at the studio to learn if we had anything new for him, and when we could furnish nothing he would frequently manufacture an item and start away upon his rounds again. One morning he paid me the usual call, and I noticed in the evening *Plain Dealer* that I (being designated as Cleveland's favorite artist) had been engaged by Frank Leslie's illustrated newspaper to go to the Crimea as staff photographer. For quite a time he alluded to me as " our favorite artist," and finally abbreviated it to " The Cleveland Pet." This pleased him greatly, because at that time there was an ugly looking " bruiser " in the city who bore that endearing title. He enjoyed making a joke at the expense of a friend; the nearer the friend and the harder the joke, the better he was pleased. When the Japanese embassy visited America to better acquaint themselves with some " things worth knowing," as touching government, commercial progress, and business methods, they brought with them a phenomenal boy known as " Japanese Tommy." This boy became a pet with the ladies in Washington society, and, in a way, quite a lion. He was the best advertised youngster this country ever knew.

Photography was entirely new to the Japanese, and some members of the embassy became interested in it. Tommy was struck with a desire to learn to make pictures and commenced the study of the art at once. Through Artemus, some photographs from my hands came to Tommy's notice, and so favorably was he impressed with them that I was asked for the formulas, and methods of production, which I was glad to give. I was rewarded by presents from Tommy, of an elegantly wrought pair of silver suspender buckles, and a number of Japanese coins. I exhibited them in my show case of photographs at the entrance of my studio, and was quite proud of them. I considered this kindness a good offset to the " Cleveland Pet " joke.

The mother of Artemus, living at Waterford, Maine, spent some time with us one summer, when we discovered that he got his drollery by inheritance. Mother and son were comrades; they enjoyed "good fun" mutually, and like overgrown children, were continually having a jolly time. They employed the given names in addressing each other; he addressing his mother as "Caroline;" she addressing him as "Charles." Mrs. Browne was humorous without realizing it; Artemus was appreciative, and watched for the very funny expressions that she

ARTEMUS WARD'S CHAIR AND TABLE.

(Now in Western Reserve Historical Society Building, Cleveland, O.)

would let fall, which he quickly picked up and carefully stored for future use. "Artemus" was devoted and loyal to "Caroline;" was loving her all the time that he was amusing himself with her unconscious humor. He would lure her to talk of the early days when his uncles and aunts came to visit them, at Waterford. "And now, Caroline," he would say, "tell me the names of them all; I am forgetful, you know, and I may have lost some of them." "Well, Charles," she would answer, "there was your uncle Daniel, and Marlboro, and Jabez, and your father, Levi, and Thadeus, and your aunts Susan and Mary and Mercy and Sarah, and that's all." "Well, wasn't that enough?" said Artemus; "but where do you come in?" "Well,

being a Farrar, I didn't come in at all; except I be counted with
your father, Levi. You remember, Charles, my father, Mr. Farrar,
kept the store at Waterford, and your father hired out to him as a
clerk.'' '' Why, Caroline,'' answered Artemus, ''how could I
remember it? That was before my time.'' '' Well, yes, ' Smarty,' ''
answered the mother, '' but I guess you've heard of it. It was
common report about Waterford years ago. Your father and I got
married, and my father took Levi in partnership, and it was Farrar
and Browne. Now, that's so, faithful! '' '' Oh, yes,'' said Artemus,
'' I remember seeing a sign over the door indicating the partnership between your father and my father. Why, what relation does
that make *us?* '' '' Now, Charles Farrar Browne, behave yourself;
be respectful to your mother; remember what the Bible says.''
'' Well, I expect I ought to; but it is so different from the *Plain
Dealer*, I don't putter with it much; you know it says a man cannot
serve two masters, and I'm a Democrat.'' Thus these two witty
personages would '' chaff '' each other by the hour. Mrs. Browne
was wonderfully proud of Charles; she said he was a strange child
from a baby, but had always been a good boy, and always good to
her. I have said that there was always a laugh or a smile upon his
face; let me record an exception. I had a dear little baby daughter
of whom he was very fond. He called her '' pappoose,'' and talked
'' baby Indian '' to her. The '' little mouse '' seemed to understand
him and accept him as a friend; her little joy was freely manifested; she tried to talk back, and delighted in clawing his nose,
which by way of encouragement was held within easy reach. Her
little feet and hands would commence talking as soon as she heard
his voice on entering the room. The little one died, and on the
morning of her death, I met him on the street. He tried to talk,
but his words turned to tears, and he wept in utter disregard of the
publicity. I was surprised to see this man of fun-making weep so
unreservedly in the open street, and it made me love him the
more.

Artemus was fond of the colored citizen, and had many friends
among them. He attended their functions in the old church on the
corner of Champlain and Seneca streets, where now stands the
Bell Telephone Exchange. It had been abandoned as a place of
worship and the lower floor occupied for manufacturing purposes,
while the large rooms upstairs were well suited for meetings,
dances, etc., and was used by the colored people as a place for their
festival meetings incident to their religious society. When a fes-

Yourn till Deth,
Artemus Ward.

tival was to be held Artemus Ward was invited, and the *Plain Dealer* was watched for with interest by the promoters of the entertainment, on the following morning. Mr. Charles Park, my brother Jack, and I, as co-admirers, frequently attended these festive occasions with Artemus. Members of the legal, medical, and the other learned professions, as well as men prominent in business who possessed a taste for unique pleasures, were generally in attendance. There were tables always daintily spread; the roast chicken and coffee unrivalled; the ice-cream, cake, and lemonade always good, of course, and the ladies of the church secured quite a harvest of silver from the output of the tables. With the colored ladies Artemus was the attraction. It was " Mistah Browne " here, and " Mistah Browne " there. " Oh, Mistah Browne, I saw you at church Sunday evening! How did you like our new minister? Are you going to say something in the paper about a certain young lady of this party who was, by far, the attraction of the evening; who left all the other young ladies in the distance? I shall be looking for it." " Good evening, Mistah Browne. I hear you going to get married. S'pose you'll never come to our parties any more then? Try a dish of my ice-cream." Then comes on a dance, after a hustle for places, and this most graceful of exercises is apparently an inheritance to young colored people. Without the training of a French master; without stilted or formal dignity of the minuet or the showy elegance of upper tendom, these young people have the gift of graceful swagger and abandon; a rollicking activity expressed in a shrug of shoulders, a twist of waist, an extending of arms, a lurch and swing, a shuffle of foot and a side scrape of same on the floor — not quite expected, but most diverting for the onlooker and a joy to the dancer. Their voices in song or hymn possess a rhythm and harmony akin to the spirit of the dance; a weaving swing of body; a treading of the musical measure with the feet, suggestive of " juba; " a suspicion of " ragtime " lurking between the lines of their sacred songs; a strain from the old plantation, diluted from what it was in the old time, but not wiped out; and a " carve dat 'possum " tinge so dear to the negro heart, and not unpleasing to other ears. These " witcheries born in the ' coon,' " and denied his white brother justifies a point in the following:

> *" We's be nearer to de Lord den de white folks,*
> *And dey knows it;*
> *See de glory gate unbarred;*
> *Walk in darkies past de guard.*
> *Bet you dollar dey wont close it;*
> *Walk in darkies tru de gate —*
> *Hark! de colored angels hollar:*
> *Go 'way white folks you too late,*
> *We's de winnin color.' "*

Without a cake-walk or dance conclusion these festivals would have been very flat. Songs and recitations were frequently given. At one time a young man of good voice sang a piece commencing:

> *" Come all young men and maidens*
> *And listen unto me."*

Which ditty carried advice to " Be true in everything ye do," etc. Artemus enjoyed this song much, and inquired of a young man sitting next him who the singer was. The young fellow replied: " Why, don't you know him? He's Bill Hamkin, the best ' Come-all-ye ' singer in town." Artemus sought an introduction to " Bill," and complimented him, saying he " had intellect into him, and was chock full of talent. You ought to be on the stage," and that's not " rote sarcastikal."

At this time, late in the fifties, Mr. Draper, a barber of the city, conceived a project of colonizing Liberia with a body of the best colored material of Cleveland and other cities of Ohio. Several meetings were called by Mr. Draper, for all persons interested in the subject to meet at the old Court House, then located in the southwest corner of the Public Square, where is now an ornamental pond spanned by a bridge. These meetings were fairly attended — out of curiosity by the colored people, and for what fun there might be in them by the whites. Mr. Draper was very sanguine about his project; said he had been studying on it a good while, and had

THE CAKE-WALK.

P. S. Ryder, Photographer, Syracuse, N. Y.

gotten the opinions of several of the brightest minds in Cleveland and they agreed that there was something in it. " Why, there's Judge Tilden," he said, " and Judge Abbey; and there's my friend Dick Parsons (meaning the Hon. Richard C. Parsons) and Mark Castle, gentlemen whom I shave; they talk it over with me every time they git in my chair. They say there may be gold mines out there, and trade and commerce will likely be established with this country; and lines of steamers running from New York to Liberia. Congress would likely make an appropriation, and our own citizens of Cleveland would contribute. Yes, gentlemen, they would come down with thousands. We can go out there and civilize those wild, crazy niggers and start gold mines. We can get good men at our backs to push us along. ' Pop-Corn ' Lewis would take stock in our mines, and carry the certificates in his basket. Some of these rising young fellows would probably like to get down on the ground floor with us. There's Mark Hanna of the West Side. And I was down on the river the other day and, in an old warehouse perched up on a high stool was John Rockefeller, a-keeping books. I hear it noised about that he is a coming man. He's very quiet, but they say he's figuring all the time. Now we want to get some of these enterprising youngsters interested in our gold mines, and next you know we'll be wearing diamonds like Jim Crocker does. Now, gentlemen, I'd like to hear from you. I want to get your views, and you are all invited to speak. The subject is one of such impor-tance you can't afford to let it pass your doors without saying a word."

The Rev. James Malvin, a patriarchal figure of good presence, his white hair and beard contrasting boldly with the dark color of his face, arose and, in a manner peculiar to himself, very deliberate of speech, winning and plausible in tone, commented upon the matter as presented by Mr. Draper. He said the aim of man seemed to be the acquirement of wealth; men wanted to get rich, they wanted to get rich quick; they couldn't let well enough alone. Said he was too old a man to start off on adventurous projects. On the whole thought he could not see the advantages as set forth by Brother Draper and, as a crusher, said that Draper reminded him of his grandfather's old musket which "scattered prodigiously," and, with the blandest of smiles, Mr. Malvin resumed his seat. Next " John Brown, the barber," an entertaining speaker, caustic and fearless, arose. He said he would like well enough to go to Liberia and get rich, like Brother Draper said they could, but

THE HOME OF THE BROWNES IN WATERFORD, MAINE.

(Occupied by them since 1805.)

thought he wouldn't shut up his shop and start right off. He
thought the colored man's paradise was right here in America.
Continuing, he said: " What kind of laws have they got in Liberia?
What kind of neighbors? What's the chance for the barbering
business? I s'pose Brother Draper could tell us that nice young
roast pigs, smothered in gravy, go cantering over the hills and are
easy to catch; that 'possums hang their tails down from the trees
so the colored man can pull them down. S'pose the soil is good for
growing sweet 'taters and watermillions — 'spec they ripen every
month. S'pose Brother Draper would like to go there and be a
king." Here John Brown looked about among the colored people,
grinned, and sat down. Joe Davis, a man of standing among the
colored people, spoke next. He gave it as his opinion that the
colored man's condition should be bettered; he was willing to go
to Liberia if he could get rich like Brother Draper said; he had
heard that some of the tribes in Liberia were savage and warlike;
as for him, if he had a good home in that country he would fight

for it — yes, he would wade in blood up to his neck to protect his home! As Joe sat down, Mr. Draper arose and said: " We have with us a gentleman who is a friend of the colored man ; a gentleman of education, a gentleman that knows more than any of us — Mr. Browne, of the *Plain Dealer.*" "Mr. Browne, wouldn't you give us your views? " he asked, turning to Artemus. On the ground of not being able to join the expedition, Artemus declined. He admitted to " having views," but feared if he attempted to give them utterance he would " scatter prodigiously." The meeting adjourned.

Artemus found pleasure in attending Methodist meetings at the colored church on the corner of Ohio and Brownell streets. In times of their revivals, which were inaugurated every winter and usually continued several weeks, these people whose fervor and earnestness were a part of their natures sometimes indulged in extravagances inconsistent with divine worship as usually conducted. But no one doubted their sincerity. They were emotional and enthusiastic, regardless of the nice proprieties of decorum in a churchly sense, and their ardor was manifest in singing and praying which was not restricted in mildness of tone. The intense natures of these good people were deeply stirred to religious excitement, and in their earnestness they forgot themselves. It was more particularly during these revival meetings that Artemus was found in attendance, and his friends of the festivals were glad to see him there, and welcomed him warmly. On one occasion when a sermon of unusual power had been preached, and Artemus had followed it closely and with eagerness, as the minister closed he rose from his seat at the extreme front, walked into the pulpit, grasped the preacher's hand and thanked him for his splendid sermon and the great good he was doing in rescuing his people from sin. He turned, walked back to his seat beside my brother with moist eyes, as my brother averred, and claimed the act was unpremeditated and with no intent of disrespect. Many white people at these times of " outpouring of grace " attended the meetings, and sometimes a convert was made among them. I knew an aged and very devout colored man who could hardly contain himself at these times, or keep in his seat. He would pace up and down the aisle, stamping and shouting. I have seen him approach the pulpit, reach his arms around it, hug it, and butt his head against it. I have heard him cry out, " Knock the side of the house off, and let de Lord come in! " then, at second thought, cry out again, " He is in here already!" "*Coming through*" was regarded as an ordeal. It was explained to me by a good Christian colored woman of whom I asked the question that the shouting, the falling in a trance condition, known by them as "having the power," is a struggle with the devil; a hard combat for release from the power of Satan, and when the poor struggling sinner conquers Satan and sin he comes into the light of Christianity a cleansed Christian. He is born again, born from darkness to light. It was no unusual thing for two or three persons to be laboring under the so-called "power" for hours, the meetings continuing sometimes until midnight, or until they would "come through."

Our evenings at the hearthstone were very enjoyable, with the glow in the grate and the wind rattling the shingles upon the roof; Artemus with his long legs stretched toward the fire, his chatter and gurgle and occasional explosions of laughter, so hearty that he would sometimes slide out of his chair and land upon the floor. He was sure to be entertaining. It always happened that he had seen some one or something during the day to please him, and he would give it to us. Down on Canal street one day he encountered a "Mrs. Mulligan" over her washtub with her dress pinned up around her waist, barefooted, and rubbing away upon her washboard, with some dirty children playing about. He accosted her with a "good morning," and inquired if she would like to do his washing, and what was her price. She straightened up, put her fists upon her hips akimbo and, with a withering stare, said: "I'm not one of those that does washings out of me own family. You're a fine gossoon! I don't even know you by eyesight." And turning to the two boys, she said: "Here, Joseph Ander, take Thomas Ander by the hand and lade him off til skule." Said Joseph Ander: "I've not had me breakfast." "Yes, and begob and ye have; ye had the blue ducks' eggs and pancakes sopped in gravy. Now be off wid yees." Artemus Ward said he thought it was time for him to go, lest she might take a fancy to wash his shirt without his taking it off. This breakfast *menu* pleased him so much that he repeated it again and again, laughing heartily at each repetition.

One evening he told us of a boarding place he had down East, where the lady in charge was possessed of great executive ability. In his words "she was a splendid manager — a pusher," while on the other hand the husband "was gifted with a great lack of stored energy." He told us that this woman was great on hash; she

Young, desired to meet him and show his " babes." It is matter of " Ward history," as shown by his published letters, that he was graciously received by the prophet and given the freedom of the city.

As a bit of " stage business " during his lectures, he was sometimes attacked with a paroxysm of coughing of such severity that a chair would be brought upon the stage in which he could sit and rest while recovering his voice. His slender form and narrow chest were suggestive of consumption. Wishing to keep his audience entertained during the interruption, he would seemingly depart from the thread of his subject and tell a story which, like the " Sweet Singer of Michigan " in her poems, generally drifted to funerals. He told of the wife of a middle-aged farmer " passing away." The neighboring women were early on hand to offer assistance and tender sympathy. Along in the forenoon, after doing the chores of the morning, the men began to call to express condolence and offer assistance. Not finding the bereaved husband, inquiry was made as to where he could be found. The women folk couldn't tell exactly, but thought he couldn't be far away. So they all filed out of the back door to look up the sorrowing man. He was not found at the barn and was nowhere in sight. One of the neighbors thought he heard a noise in the well, and, on looking down, saw the bereaved one and asked what he was doing down there. To which he replied that his wife's death had made rather a broken day, and he thought it would be a good time to clean out the well. Presently he climbed up out of the well and received with composure the assurances of sympathy from his neighbors. They all told him they would be glad to render him any needed assistance, and he had only to tell them how they could serve him. One of the neighbors had recently purchased a large silver hunting case watch which the mourner had seen and admired, and who made bold to ask for the loan of the coveted timepiece to wear at the funeral. The owner cheerfully unhooked the stout steel chain from his vest and handed it over. During the funeral services the chief mourner was seen to snap the watch open every few minutes, learn the time, and snap it shut in a manner that attracted the attention of the entire congregation. When the cortege reached the cemetery and the bearers were about to lower the coffin into the grave, he again took out the watch, opened it and held it open, watching the minute hand closely, and when the box was heard to strike the bottom he snapped the case down in a dramatic manner

New York, Feb 2/61

Dear Charlie:

Your last came
duly to hand.

I haven't seen Brown yet-
-called once but he wasn't
in. Shall see him sure.

Tell Jule I have "gone back
on" suppers, the vigorous meals
I absorb at 3 p.m. daily being entirely adequate for my
sustenance. I "reach for the
bread" just as I did in the
palmy days of Wilsons tavern,
and pour out my own tea —
scolded a waiter the other night
pretty bad, but he excused me

I go East first of March
to see Caroline. Going or coming I shall visit Willimantic.
Shall go to "Woosup" likewise.

ANOTHER LETTER TO CHAS. E. WILSON FROM ARTEMUS WARD.

as I must see "Ossy" and
Jenny.

Caroline is getting reconciled to
my change of location. Her
late letters are quite cheerful.

Now I blush as I write
it— I feel I am coming it
altogether too strong on you—but
do hunt up my "Three Tigers
of the Cleveland Press" and send
it on in a letter. The piece was
not in the bundle I so sent. The
piece is valuable to me. In short,
without the piece I shall be
unhappy, and prithee, send her
on. Set some of the boys in the
mailing department to work
hunting it up, and my children's
children shall lisp your name
with heartfelt affection. Bully Boy!

As I was quietly taking some
coffee and cakes with Henry Ward

Beecher at Smith's in Chatham
Street the other night; after the
Bowery was out, he accidentally
alluded to you. "Wilson," says
he, "is a young man of much
promise. He is a good bookkeepist
as his balance sheets are always
correct: I like Wilson." He also
spoke of Lefs but I am sorry
to say he was not very complemen=
tary. "Lester," says Mr. Beecher,
"will come to the gallus in
about two years, if he keeps on
"What do you think of Brokenshire,
Henry?" says I. "A good man,
Sir," said Mr. Beecher—"a very
good man indeed tho' he's a d—d
Englishman." On getting up
from the table Mr. Beecher
insisted on allowing me to pay
for the coffee and cakes—12 cents.
        I anticipate considerable fun

in my forthcoming trip to the
East; tho. my stay will necessarily
be short.

By the way, love to the ever
blooming Briggs. Shall write him
soon. Did he get the $16,000,000
and box of jewels I sent him
the other day?

Send the "Tigers." I shall
soon cease troubling you I hope.
And now farewell. A fond
embrace. A few natural tears
and some wild groans! There,
there, it's over now. Adoo! adoo!

Yours Ever,

A. Ward.

and announced, " It was just twenty minutes past two when we got her in." The roars of applause which greeted this story were construed by Artemus as an encore, to which after rising, bowing, smiling, and reseating he would respond by relating the following, which he certified to as being as true as the one just told: In a small village where there was no undertaker, a death had occurred and a coffin was wanted, and one of the citizens who was going to town was entrusted to secure one. This man was extremely fond of limburger cheese and could not resist purchasing a few pounds. The sample he got was very talented, in a way, and he did not wish to carry it about with him, so he went to the express office to ship it home. But the agent declined to receive it, on the ground of its being " too loud." A happy thought struck him and he hied away to the undertaker's shop and, with his prize well wrapped in repeated papers, put it in the coffin to be sent to the train for the first run west. Before taking his seat in the coach to return home he looked into the baggage car and found " it " was on board. Before reaching the home station he sauntered into the baggage car, found the baggage master with his head sticking out of the side door and the casket placed by the open back door of the car. He looked at it in an interested way, and was turning to walk back when the " trunk smasher " asked him: " Does that belong to you?" " Yes," said the passenger. " Any relation?" asked the baggage man. " Wife," was the response. " Well," said the smasher, with head reached well out, " she ain't in no *trance* ! "

Artemus learned the printer's trade in the Oxford County *Advertiser* office, Norway, Maine. He had a brother, Cyrus, who was also a printer, having learned his trade in the same office and afterwards become editor of the New Bedford *Standard*. Like Artemus he was a humorist, and more droll than his brother because of a peculiar drawling voice which emphasized his drollery. He died some years before Artemus. Dr. J. C. Gallison, of Franklin, Mass., also learned the printer's trade in the *Advertiser* office. Artemus preceded him and had left something of his fame for the new boy to look up to. He says: " I was a mere boy — a very young man. I regarded Charley Browne with mingled worship and awe — for had he not traveled?" It was related of Artemus that while " devil " on the *Advertiser* he became disgusted because of the continual boasting of the rival paper about a new window that had been put in and the week following had had the casing painted, and other small matters that were announced certifying to the enterprise of the establishment.   Artemus wrote and the *Advertiser* published this item: " We have bored a new hole in the sink and put a bran new slop pail under it.   What will the hell-hounds of the other office say to that?"

The following letter is from Dr. Gallison to the *Advertiser:*

DEAR ADVERTISER: I was very much interested in Dr. Bradbury's account of the life of Artemus Ward in Norway. And right here let me express my appreciation of the doctor's wonderful sketches of " Norway in the Forties." I have read them with unflagging interest and ever-increasing wonder at the accuracy and evidence of painstaking research — a labor of love surely, but one whose results should be preserved in a more permanent form than in the columns of a weekly newspaper. The old residents of the town owe a debt of gratitude to the author of " Norway in the Forties." I was much amused by the doctor's description of the little dingy room occupied by Artemus in the old *Advertiser* office. How well I recollect the room! It was for a long time *my* " den " in Norway, while printer's devil in the now famous office. A rickety old cord bedstead, rheumatic and complaining; a straw " tick " of very ancient lineage — the very one upon which Artemus reposed his lengthy limbs; a bottomless chair, a fragment of looking-glass pasted upon the wall, a bottle or two for candlesticks made up the furnishing of the room. The remaining space was occupied by a large table or bench upon which was kept the spare paper for job work and the *Anvertiser* for the coming week. Disabled old " galleys," ancient " cases," the " hell-box," the " ribs and trucks " of a defunct hand-press — over which we tumbled dark nights — filled the little room until there was barely space enough for the repose of the lamps of the office. I well recollect a visit made to the *Advertiser* office by Artemus and his brother Cyrus. As a boy I neglected my " stick " and " copy " to listen to the rich, rare and racy fun of the brothers, sitting in the corner sanctum of " Boss " Millett, who was by no means slow in contributing his share of the quiet humor and brilliant wit. The whole office was in an uproar of broad laughter, and I can see the genial Charlie Thompson, the foreman, his long figure convulsed with merriment. Artemus was very droll, but to my mind the brother with his drawling voice was some laps ahead. It was about this time that Mark H. Dunnell was a candidate for representative to the legislature from Norway. He made " the speech of his life " one evening in Denison's Hall, in which he set forth in lurid colors the fearful condition of the country in general and of Norway in particular. Artemus reported the speech for the *Advertiser*, and a more telling adverse report was never written. It abounded in ridicule, rollicking fun, and side-splitting jokes. It convulsed the town, and came near defeating the doughty Mark. Referring to Ward's traveling abroad, the doctor says: " An old schoolmate of his in Waterford, Horace Maxfield, son of the old stage driver Maxfield, accompanied him and was with him through his last illness and death. Maxfield brought home with him some admission tickets which had been used for entrance to his lectures. These were distributed among Ward's immediate friends." The doctor further says: " I have one of these tickets, which, together with my old printer's rule, is in the drawer of the desk at which I am writing, and which I keep as relics — as mementos of Artemus and the old days."

In the days when Cyrus Browne and his brother, Charles Farrar Browne, better known as " Artemus Ward," lived in Waterford,
" the little Maine village that nestled among the hills and never did
anything else but nestle," Charles delighted to play practical jokes
on Cyrus.   Charles came home one freezing night, says the narrator
of the following prank in the Boston *Herald*, at an hour that would
be thought early in a metropolis, but was not so considered in
Waterford.   The family were sleeping soundly in the warm comfort of their beds when the future showman halted under the
window of Cyrus, and raised an alarm.

"Cy! oh, Cy! Come out here, Cy!"

After a time Cyrus appeared at the window.   "What do you
want?" he demanded through the crack he had opened.

"I want you to come down!" with great earnestness.   "I
want to ask you a question, Cy."

"Oh, go 'way!" said Cyrus, his teeth chattering in the awful
cold.   "It's only one of your jokes."

"Really, Cy, it's a very important question," persisted Charles
with increased earnestness.   "It's a solemn thing, and I want you
to come down, Cy; I want you bad."

Finally, after grumbling and expostulating, Cyrus slipped on
some clothes and came reluctantly downstairs and out into the
arctic cold.   "Now what in the world is it that you want?" he
asked.

Charles came up close, laid his hands on his brother's shivering
shoulders, and in that voice of plaintive solemnity, which in after
years moved so many people to mirth, said:

"I want to ask you, Cy, if you think slavery is wrong?"

From Charles E. Wilson, now of Hartford, Conn., I get the
following touching Artemus's wanderings:

"Being of a roving disposition, he left the *Advertiser*, of
Norway, Maine.   He worked for a time at Skowhegan and at Gard-
iner, Maine, and later drifted down to Boston, where he obtained a
situation in the composing-room of the *Carpet Bag*, published by
Benj. P. Shillaber (Mrs. Partington).   While employed in this
office he wrote his first article of any pretension and shoved the copy
under Shillaber's sanctum door.   He was much gratified a few days
later to see the copy come into the composing-room to be " set up,"
and being thus encouraged he wrote another article, rather historical in character, making no attempt to be funny, and this also
went under the sanctum door.   Neither of these articles was

signed, but Shillaber was satisfied that they were written by some one in the office, and accordingly made inquiry, which resulted in Browne's acknowledging that he wrote them. Shillaber patted him on the back, metaphorically, told him he manifestly had ability and encouraged him to make literary work a study and profession. While in the *Carpet Bag* office Artemus told me, as an instance of Mr. Shillaber's humor, that one evening a fire broke out near their office and all dropped their cases to go to the conflagration. Shillaber was ready to go first, and as he was going out of the door called back, " Boys, look out for your lights! " And on returning, a couple of hours later, completed the sentence by adding, " and your livers." After leaving the *Carpet Bag* office he tramped west, bringing up after a time at Cincinnati, where he worked a few days upon the Cincinnati papers. Noticing one day in one of the local papers an advertisement, " School teacher wanted," at a small town in Kentucky, near Cincinnati, he answered it and secured the position, but only taught the school one week. There were several big boys in the school, and he learned from local gossips that these young toughs had " licked " every schoolmaster that had attempted to " keep school " there for several years previous. As he was not particularly robust, and had never studied the " noble art " of self-defense he concluded the climate of that Kentucky village would not exactly suit him. At the close of school on Friday night he packed his modest wardrobe in his down-east carpet bag and, without waiting to collect his week's pay, started early Saturday morning for Cincinnati. He did not remain there long, however, but pushed along up the Cincinnati, Hamilton & Dayton Railway, stopped a short time in Dayton, thence on to Springfield, where he obtained a situation as compositor and remained several weeks. Major W. W. Armstrong, publisher of the Tiffin *Advertiser* along in the fifties, engaged Artemus for his paper, temporarily, to fill a sick man's place. Artemus walked from Sandusky to Tiffin, a distance of thirty-four miles, to take the job. The major says he reached Tiffin late in the day, clad in a long linen duster, a shilling chip hat, and his carpet bag, and said he was hungry and weary, but jolly; considered the feat a good joke. When he came again, a few years later, to exhibit his " Moral Snaix and Wax Works " at Webster Hall, he averred that a prejudiced citizen smashed the face of Judas Iscariot with a brick, declaring the " betrayer " could never again show his ugly mug in Seneca County. His next stopping place was at Toledo, where he

ARTEMUS WARD
AMONG THE MORMONS.

BRAINARD'S HALL!
CLEVELAND, OHIO,
TUESDAY AND WEDNESDAY, MAY 9TH AND 10TH.

HIS PROGRAMME.

I.

The Music on the Grand Piano will comprise selections from "Don Sebastian;" "Mary had a little Lamb" (with mint sauce variations); "Dearest, whenest thou slumberest dostest thou dreamest of me?" "Dear Mother, I've come Home to Die by request;" and the entirely new Opera of "Faust."

II.

A light and airy Preamble by the Lecturer, with some jokes. ·(N. B.—ARTEMUS WARD will call on citizens at their private residences and explain these jokes, if necessary.)

III.

At Sea.—The Steamer Ariel. Disgraceful treatment of the passengers, who are obliged to go forward to smoke pipes, while the steamer herself is allowed two Smoke Pipes amid-ships. Isthmus of Panama. Interesting interview with old Panama himself, who makes all the hats. Old Pan is a likely sort of man .

IV.

The Land of Gold.—San Francisco. City with a vigilant government. Miners allowed to vote. Old inhabitants so rich that they have legs with golden calves to them.

V.

Washoe, the Land of Silver.—Good quarters to be found there. Playful population, fond of high-low-jack and homicide. Silver lying around loose. Thefts of it termed silver-guilt.

VI.

The Desert.—In the act of howling. Wild goats abound on the desert, however. Their kids are white, and Artemus Ward will wear a pair of them.

VII.

Great Salt Lake City.—A Bird's-eye view, with some entirely serious descriptive talk.

VIII.

The West Side of Main Street.—The Salt Lake Hotel, &c. Stage just come in from its overland route and retreat from the Indians. Temperance House. No bar nearer than Salt Lake sand bars. Miners in shirts like Artemus Ward his Programme—they are read and will wash

IX.

The East Side of Main Street.—The State House and things. The Post Office also. A few years ago an enterprising Mormon started an opposition Post Office, and by selling three cent stamps for two cents, tried to run the regular Post Office out of own. He is now a flourishing Outcast in Pennsylvania, and owns Oil Wells.

X.

The Mormon Theatre.—By the kind consent of many families, Artemus Ward acted Richard III., or Old Dick the Three, at this Theatre one night, and so brilliant was his success—so grand and moving was the impersonation, that an hour before he had finished there was only one man in the audience, and he would have left it if he had not got himself entangled with the benches, which prevented him making his escape. This is important if true.

PROGRAMME OF ARTEMUS WARD'S MORMON LECTURE.

XI.

Brigham Young's Houses.—Brigham's Wives live in these houses. They live well at Brigham's. the following being the usual

Bill of Fare.

SOUPS, &c.	COLD.
Matrimonial Stews (*with pretty pickles.*)	Raw Dog (*a la Injun*).
FISH.—Salt Lake Gudgeon.	Tongue (*lots of it.*)
ROAST.	VEGETABLES.
Brigham's Lamb (*Sauce piquante.*)	Cabbage-head, Some Pumpkins, &c.
Minced Hearts (*Mormon style.*)	
BROILED.	DESSERT.
Domestic Broils (*Family Style*).	Apples of discord, a great many Pairs.
ENTREES.—Little Deers.	Mormon Sweet-Hearts, Jumbles, &c.

XII.

Heber C. Kimball's Harem.—Mr. Kimball is a kind husband and a numerous father.

Selections for the Grand Piano......................**Mr. Forrester**

Mr. Forrester once boarded in the same street with Gottschalk. The man who kept the boarding house remembers it

---

XIII.

The Tabernacle.—The Mormon Meeting House. One of the Elders who preaches here actually plays in Comedy at the Theatre. We should like to know what Mr. Warren thinks of this. Brigham's son isn't an Elder. He's a Younger.

XIV

The Temple as it is.

XV

The Temple as it is to be.

XVI.

The Great Salt Lake. An inland sea of brine. There are no boats in this lake, but a Mormon lives near by who says he has a whole "raft of wives."

XVII.

The Endowment House. Here is where disciples of Mormonism are initiated. The Mormon's religion is singular, and his wives are plural.

XVIII.

The Plains Again.—A more cheerful view. A tribute to the memory of a celebrated Indian Chief—"Listen to these tears!"

XIX.

Echo Canon.—A rough bluff sort of affair. Great Echo. When Artemus Ward went through, he heard the echoes of some things the Indians said there about four years and a half ago

XX.

Brigham Young and his Wives.—The pretty girls in Utah mostly marry Young

☞ Those of the audience who do not feel offended with Artemus Ward are cordially invited to call upon him, often, at his fine new house in Chicago. His house is on the right hand side as you cross the Ferry, and may be easily distinguished from the other houses by its having a Cupola and a Mortgage on it.

LOST—A small boy named Augustus Smith. Little Augustas went to hear Artemus Ward, and wanted to go again very much. His parents unwisely refused him that pleasure, whereupon Augustus became moody and refused meat victuals. He soon after disappeared. Was last seen reading the National Intelligencer in a mournful manner in the Village church-yard at N—— Information may be sent to Mr. Smith of Chicago and vicinity.

ANSWERS TO CORRESPONDENTS.

SACCHARISSA.—"I have no Home; where shall I go?" If you want a "Home, Sweet Home," you had better go on a Sugar Plantation.

SHARKEY.—"How can a fellow get a free passage on one of the North River Boats?" Any Judge of a Criminal Court can give you one—as far as Sing Sing.

CONSCRIPT (Canada).—"Do they think of me at home, do they ever think of ?" No; but they do at the Provost-Marshal's-Office.

LAURA MATILDA.—"I have an unfortunate tendency, even on trivial occasions, to shed tears. How can I prevent it?" Lock up the shed.

ALFRED.—"Where, O where can the weary soul find rest?" We don't know. You can get board in —— Street, however, for five dollars a week.

TRAVELER.—"How long was Artemus Ward in California?" Five feet ten-and-a-half.

BOUNTY JUMPER (Canada).—"Had I better come back to the States?" Certainly not by all means. You had better hang yourself with a piece of the Canada Line.

LOYAL.—"I wish to procure some trophies of the present rebellion; battle flags, &c. How can I do so?" One very good way is to shoulder a gun and go and take them.

SPECULATOR.—"Is Petroleum frequent in caves?" No: but caves are frequent in Petroleum.

CITIZEN.—"I am getting bald. What will make my hair come out?" Oil of Vitriol will make all your hair come out.

INQUIRER.—"I am desirous of becoming a Mormon: what shall I do first?" First get good common sense, and then you won't want to be a Mormon.

COUNTRYMAN.—"Are there any Petroleum Whales?" No; but there are plenty of Petroleum Sharks.

RULES OF THIS HOUSE.

.*. Children in arms not admitted, if the Arms are loaded.

.*. Children under one year of age not admitted, unless accompanied by their parents or guardians.

.*. Ladies or gentlemen will please report any negligence or disobedience on the part of the Lecturer.

.*. Artemus Ward will not be responsible for money, jewelry or other valuables, unless left with him—to be returned in a week or so.

.*. The manager will not be responsible for any debts of his own contracting.

.*. If the audience do not leave the Hall when this entertainment is over, they will be put out by the police.

.*. Persons who think they will enjoy themselves more by leaving the Hall early in the evening, are requested to do so with as little noise as possible.

.*. For particulars see Posters and Newspaper Advertisements.

.*. Cards of Admission 50 cts. Parquette and Front Chairs in Dress Circle, 75 cts. Admission to Matinee, on Saturday afternoon, 25 cts., to all parts of the house.

.*. Mr. CARLETON, Publisher, New York, has in press, for speedy publication, Mr. Ward's new book: "ARTEMUS WARD AMONG THE MORMONS," splendidly illustrated with humorous drawings. Uniform with "Artemus Ward, His Book."

secured the position of market reporter on the Toledo *Commercial*. It was on this paper that his work as writer really commenced. When James D. Cleveland (later Judge Cleveland), who had held the position of city editor on the *Plain Dealer*, was called as assistant clerk to the United States District Court, Artemus Ward was called to fill his chair. How well he filled it is generally known in Cleveland and throughout the country.

From a letter of date March 15, 1867, written by Albion Chadbourne, of London, England (formerly of Waterford), to Daniel Browne, of Waterford, Maine, an uncle of Artemus, I get information of interest as follows: Mr. Chadbourne, a close friend of Artemus in the early days of his coming, was active in introducing him among his friends and especially in making his *début* a success; took with him a good number of friends to the lecture with a view to encouraging and applauding him, but says he found it quite unnecessary, as his reception was an ovation. Chadbourne and his friends had difficulty in getting into the hall, even, so crowded was it. Never had an American visited London as a stranger who immediately found his way to the favor and friendship of the English people as did Artemus. His popularity was unprecedented. He was soon admitted to membership of a club of authors and artists, and while in London spent many happy hours with them. At the residence of Mr. Millward, one of the foremost members of the club, Artemus spent his first evening in London, and, after his death, his remains were brought from Southampton to Mr. Millward's residence and lay in state until his burial, which occurred in the chapel at Kensel Green, where all which was mortal of that sunny nature lies in a tomb by itself. Mr. Chadbourne, one of the pall-bearers, says that many honest tears were shed in the circle of friends who surrounded his grave. (The remains have since been removed and interred in the family lot at Waterford, Maine.)

Of Artemus Ward, says John Paul Jones, of Toledo, a gentleman of infinite appreciation: "Your mention of ' A. Ward's ' lecture on the Mormons brings to mind the first time I ever heard Artemus — at Bryan Hall, Chicago. An audience of over three thousand testified to his popularity, which was fully deserved. Little did I then think I should ever meet him in Toledo and know him as I did afterwards. He nearly killed me here with his panorama and stories of the Mormons. But during a three-hours' call at my office with a bevy of young ladies to witness an exhibition by our fire department in testing a new engine in front of the Island House, his wit was more than a match for the squirt of the water — quite as forceful and continuous. It was a treat I have cherished as among the choicest of my recollections of ' Artemus.' "

A letter from Artemus Ward to his old friend, Charles W. Coe, follows here:

WATERFORD, OXFORD CO., MAINE,
June 2, '66.

MY DEAR CHARLIE COE,
            of Cleveland, O.

Your favor was forwarded me here from New York. I was sincerely glad to hear from you, and the fact of my not writing you for so long a time was due to negligence solely, and I can't say fairer than that. I saw, as you suppose, your friend Ike at Denver. He was drunk, but that I understood was his popular condition. He obtained five tickets for my lecture from me, remarking that he would pay me the following day. I feel confident that he would have done so, if he had done so. Ike, in short, is in a bad way. A good fellow, I fancy, but whiskey has done for him.

I was lucky in California, as you will be glad to hear, I know. I am located here with my mother for two months, when I shall return to New York. I am writing a book on my travels, and may try to establish myself permanently in the fall with a pictorial entertainment on the Mormons. My brother died a few weeks since. He had long been an invalid, though he bore his sufferings heroically. I speak with a brother's fondness and partiality, but he was a man of singular brilliancy and had a very large heart. This event, which is a very sad one to me, cuts our little family down to my dear old mother and myself. I want to come and see you but fear I shall not find time this season. Write me here soon, and with much love to your family and with many fervent wishes for your prosperity, believe me, dear Charlie,

Always your old friend,
C. F. BROWNE.

Come down here this summer. Why not?

Dear Artemus! his mission was to " tickle the ribs " of the world, and the world stood the tickling right cheerfully.

In Cleveland is an Artemus Ward Club. Its membership is composed exclusively of newspaper men of the city, and his memory is kept green by his old associates.

" *Is he gone to the land of no laughter,*
This man who made mirth for us all? "

CHAPTER XXII.

WAR OF THE REBELLION.

When the war of the Rebellion came and a call for men was made and thousands of young men were offering themselves to the government — to their country, I was stirred with a desire to do something. While because of physical defects I could not be accepted as a soldier, yet I could manifest my friendliness to the cause and the boys who were going, in another way. I advertised that all young men going to the front not having a photograph to leave with their mothers should come to me and get one free of charge. So cordially and numerously was my invitation accepted that I found myself very busy for several weeks. I worked exclusively for the soldier boys, declining to receive orders or money for other work, explaining to my regular customers that I felt under a patriotic obligation to serve the boys before all others.

It came to pass that many of those boys did not return, and in many instances those hastily made photographs were valued above price. The thanks I received from mothers, brothers, sisters, and fathers were many. In those days of preparation companies of soldiers were sent in from surrounding towns to be drilled in camp, and from our camps in Cleveland were sent to other camps nearer the front. Every day or two new regiments went marching through our streets from camp to cars, headed for the conflict. It was no uncommon thing to see marching beside a young soldier, in the ranks, his mother, his sister, or possibly his sweetheart, to have a last few words of farewell; a hand within a hand, a hand resting upon the arm of a dear boy, possibly going to his death; the giving, at the moment of separation, a pocket Bible, a finger ring, a trinket of some sort as a mascot, with a wish that was a prayer, were trying incidents, likely to bring a lump to the throat of a sympathetic beholder. By and by, some poor wounded boy in blue would be seen coming up from the train in a baggage wagon going to the hospital, or, if a resident, possibly returning to his mother or his wife. I remember one morning a sturdy soldier named Tillotson was brought up from the depot

EX-PRESIDENT JAMES A. GARFIELD.

(First photograph taken after his nomination.)

lying upon a stretcher in a baggage wagon (this was before ambulances), which was backed up to the entrance door of the Weddell House, and, while preparations were making for his removal from the wagon to the hotel, he lay there patiently upon his back, holding an umbrella over his face to keep the sun off. This was my first sight of a wounded soldier and is distinctly remembered. As time wore on these happenings were more frequent, wounded men came home to be nursed and the dead sent home to be buried. This was war and its results, a realization mournfully and bitterly experienced in many homes. In these times I was kept very busy. I had never a leisure hour, the activity of war times was upon us all, and thousands upon thousands of photographs did I make to be sent to the boys at the front, in camp, and in the hospitals. Many sad and tender histories, unpublished, unknown save to the actors, could be woven about those photographs. When a lucky soldier would receive from home a letter, a parcel or photograph his comrades would share the reading; it was a letter from home, from a comrade's home if not their own; a mother or a sister had written it. To every man so fortunate as to listen to loving expressions from some other fellow's home there came a touch of sympathy, and a mental glimpse of his own home came as a pleasing memory. Many poor fellows home on sick furlough were besieged by friends for photographs.

I remember well when Colonel Garfield (later general, senator, president, and martyr) came to my gallery for a sitting. Through the bronzed complexion was the pallor of the invalid. He was home on sick leave, and though ill his heart was strong, and the genial, cheerful air so characteristic of him was present. As I was sitting him he remarked that he would about as soon stand before a gun; said it gave him the uncomfortable feeling of being aimed at to have a camera pointed toward him. I was much impressed with him. He was truly the soldier and gentleman. His genial kindness was a distinguishing trait. It was my good fortune to see him often and know him through the rest of his life. The train-master at the Union Depot at Cleveland told me how he was beloved by the employes about the depot. He always had a kind word for everyone. When some subject was discussed that was beyond them, it was agreed to leave it to General Garfield, and when he came again, and there was a minute to spare, his opinion was sought and the question quickly decided. He was their authority and teacher, in a hasty fashion. He was truly the common man's friend. It was told of him that once in Ithaca, New York, he was to deliver a lecture, and walking through the street with one of the most prominent citizens, who was entertaining him at his home, he espied a man with overalls on and paint pot in hand who was evidently trying to pass unnoticed. The general excused himself from his escort a moment and made for the painter. "Why, hello, Charley!" he cried, "I am very glad to see you," shaking him by the hand meanwhile. As the painter passed on, in happy confusion, Garfield turned to his escort and said: "That is one of the bravest men I ever knew. He was in my regiment and one of my best fighters." "Charley" was a recognized hero after that.

During the fall of Garfield's campaign for the presidency, Lawnfield, his home at Mentor, was a very busy place. Many train loads of visitors from Cleveland and other towns, cities, and states came to pay visits and pledge loyalty to him. There was a day for first-voters, a business men's day, a workingmen's day, soldiers' day, Germans' day, colored men's day, women's day, and there were many "go-as-you-please" delegations without distinctive names, but all loyal friends. I frequently went with these delegations, as did many other Clevelanders. The Lake Shore & Michigan Southern Railway ran through Mentor, the trains stopping at a lane which led up to Lawnfield, about three-quarters of a mile from his residence, and was known that year (1880) as Delegation Road, because all visitors by rail walked up from the train by that route. An office building in the rear of the Garfield home was called the "Workshop." It was the general's headquarters for committee and managers' work, telegraph office, and reporters' rooms. On arrival of these delegations they formed upon the lawn, and some leading spirit of the party addressed the general,

The Elton Studio, Photographers, Cleveland, O.

REVERIE.

on crutches, so crippled from rheumatism that he walked with much difficulty. I noticed him again when, some twenty minutes after all the others had arrived, he came hobbling along hurrying to hear the general's address of welcome. When the afternoon was in the wane and the delegation was preparing for its return to the train, I saw the old man starting ahead that he might reach the train by the time his crowd got there. I called the general's attention to the man who had performed that painful trip to see the man for whom he should cast his vote for president, and Garfield without

pledging for his party its loyalty and support. Then from the general came a response which was a model of oratory. The opposing party watched in vain for a word which might be turned against him.

The train carrying the colored delegation, I remember, was a merry one. The colored man loved the general. A band of music, all colored players, was a feature of this excursion. I rode in the car with the music, and wondered whether the roof of the car or my ear-drums would yield first. As the train reached Delegation Road and was unloaded of its passengers, I noticed an aged colored man

W. J. Bogart, Photographer, Toronto, Canada.

SUNSHINE GIRL.

making any show of the act hastily called a man from the stable, told him to hitch up his buggy as quickly as possible, overtake the old colored man and drive him to the cars; and that was the Garfield of it. The poor, old, crippled man received that kindly attention gratefully. The incident did not appear in the papers next day under a big type heading; it takes its first publication here.

Of the many soldiers who visited my studio there are some to be especially remembered. After Garfield's election to the presidency, a soldier accompanied by a friend came into my studio one day and wanted a photograph of Garfield, and I handed out a few for selection. The soldier took one in his hand and said: " That's good of Jim." The friend said, " You'd hardly dare call him Jim, now he is president." " Of course I would; I always called him Jim and always will. We were boys together in school and on the farm. We were neighbors and friends. I am perfectly free to call him Jim, and he is perfectly willing to have me. I called him colonel in the army, like the other boys, not to be too familiar; but he knows, and I know."

I was in Washington at the time of Garfield's inauguration, and saw him turn and kiss his old mother when the ceremony was ended, and I think I have loved him more since that day.

On the day after his nomination, while on the way to Cleveland I wired my congratulations to him upon his train, and asked for photograph sittings the following morning. The immense crowd at the depot on the arrival of his train, and at the Kennard House, where he was taken by the reception committee, prevented my seeing him that night. A prominent gentleman and political friend insisted upon taking him to his residence that night, and a few military and political men were invited to breakfast with him next morning. Full of the belief that the roof which covered Garfield was free and not exclusive from approach by any American citizen, I went in the morning with a carriage to drive him down to my photographic establishment directly after breakfast. At the door I inquired for the gentleman of the house that I might make known the purpose of my visit. The sleek colored man told me he was not down yet; but, he added, " the General is down," and ushered me into the parlor, where I found Garfield in conversation with a newspaper man who was also his college mate. My presence was not considered an intrusion by either and they talked freely. Garfield said his nomination was in the way of a hardship to him; that his political career was interrupted and thwarted; he thought his best usefulness would have been achieved by a few years more in the senate, but, although it had come before he felt ready for it, he must accept and do his best.   This I was surprised to hear, thinking the highest honor which could be bestowed by the people of America to one of their number was always welcome.   As the editor released him, he turned to me and said he had received my telegram, but did not see his way clear to give me sittings, as he was to have a reception at the Kennard House at nine o'clock.   The breakfast party had now arrived, and the host with the ladies of his family had come down from their rooms above to meet their guests. They came too soon for my escape, and they stood between me and my hat and umbrella.   The splendid host greeted with warm welcome his morning guests.   He did not understand the object of my visit and regarded it an intrusion, and the heartiness of his welcome was not extended to me.   His manner was to my mind objectionable and could not be overlooked by his guest of honor. It won for me the sittings I desired, and moved the sympathetic kindliness of the man who had consideration for another man under embarrassment.   Garfield found it possible to stop at my gallery and pose for the first sitting after his nomination for president, while the reception waited.   I was at my old home in Ithaca, visiting my mother, when the news of the assassination was flashed through the land.   I could not at first believe the truthfulness of the report.   I hurried to the telegraph office for news, and to learn of his condition.   I was referred by the operator to the publication office of the principal newspaper.   There I found a bulletin announcing the shooting, but of his condition nothing could be learned.   I was told by a young man in charge of the business office whom I did not know that an " extra " would be issued at four o'clock; it was then half-past two.   I said, " You evidently have news if you are to issue an extra at four o'clock.   If you are holding it you are treating your fellow citizens unfairly."   I inquired for the proprietor and was told he was not in.   Filled with impatience and indignation at the young man's indifference and such slow business methods, I told the young man that forty years before I was printer's " devil " in that office, and was sorry to feel I was not fairly treated.   I thought any American citizen was entitled to the latest news of a dying president.   I went back to the telegraph office, but got no news.   The operators explained that they got their dispatches over a single wire from Sayre, Pa., a station near Elmira, N. Y., and for some reason they were very slow.   I asked how early the office would be opened on the morrow, which was Sunday. His reply was prompt, " Oh, we are never open Sundays." I inquired as to *why* it was not opened. He said it was not their custom, that it was not required of him to keep it open, that he was not paid for being there, and he wanted the day to himself. I found that three dollars would keep him at his post through the day, so I secured his services and the office was mine for that day. I visited it every half hour, but got no news of the wounded president. I wondered why, in 1881, the telegraphic service was so defective as to be unable to give us news of so important a nature. During the long days and nights of his suffering at the White House in Washington it was deemed unwise to allow his family to visit him. Dr. D. W. Bliss, his physician, an old friend of my own, with whom I had correspondence, told me in reply to an inquiry that he saw no objection to having the president's mother's portrait hung in his sick room. I prepared one and sent it for that purpose. I was afterward told he found much comfort in looking at the dear old face of her who had been his guide and encouragement in his early struggles for an education and a career.

The greatest compliment that ever came to me, one which I can never forget but shall cherish always, came from the martyred President, and I beg indulgence to present it here in the following clipping:

[From *Success*, June, 1900.]

After photographing over a million faces, including those of several presidents of the United States, James F. Ryder has retired from business in Cleveland, Ohio, and is now enjoying the rest which may fairly be said to have been earned after an active career of half a century.

To a representative of *Success*, who called on him the other day, in his Euclid avenue home, Mr. Ryder said: " The greatest compliment ever paid me came from James A. Garfield, and was entirely unexpected. The general was making a speech to the students of a business college, in Washington, on the subject, ' Success,' when he made use of the following language, which, as you may imagine, did me a great amount of good:

" Only yesterday, on my way here, I learned a fact which I will give you to show how, by attending to things and putting your mind to the work, you may reach success. A few days ago, in the city of Boston, there was held an exhibition of photography, and to the great surprise of New England it turned out that Mr. Ryder, a photographer from Cleveland, Ohio, took the prize for the best photography in America. But how did this happen? I will tell you. This Cleveland photographer happened to read in a German paper of a process practiced by the artists of Bohemia — a process of touching up the negative with the finest instruments, thus removing all chemical imperfections from the negative itself. Reading this, he sent for one of these artists, and at length succeeded in bringing the art of Bohemia into the service of his own profession.

"The patient German sat down with his lenses, and, bringing a strong clear light upon these negatives, working with the finest instruments, rounding and strengthening the outlines, was able, at length, to print from the negative a photograph more perfect than any I have seen with an India ink finish. And so Mr. Ryder took the prize. Why not? It was no mystery; it was simply taking time by the forelock, securing the best aid in his business, and bringing to bear the force of an energetic mind to attain the best possible results. That is the only way, young ladies and gentlemen, in which success is gained. These men succeed because they deserve success. Their results are wrought out; they do not come to hand already made. Poets may be born, but success is made."

P. S. Ryder, Photographer, Syracuse, N. Y.

"WHAT BOY IS THAT?"

CHAPTER XXIII.

AS A PUBLISHER.

In 1872 I moved from my old location at the corner of Superior and Bank streets to 239 Superior street, where I fitted up a fine establishment as an art store and photograph gallery combined. The large exhibition window in front, approached by a vestibule entrance through graceful double columns where was always a fine exhibit of interesting pictures, became a pleasant attraction to passers-by and was well patronized by lovers of art objects. On entering the store the visitor found much to please the eye. At the rear of the store, passing through an entrance to the right, was a special exhibition room for paintings where good objects of art were always to be found. There many art lovers and students spent hours in admiring and studying. It was regarded a privilege and pleasure to find in Cleveland so good a collection always on free exhibition. From surrounding cities and strangers visiting Cleveland, large numbers were entertained.

A. M. Willard, of Wellington, Ohio, sent up to me one day a pair of paintings to be framed. I placed them on exhibition in my show window. I had a constant crowd looking at them. All that crowd were delighted with the story that pair of pictures told. A boy had hitched up, to a wagon of his own make, the big family dog, and as passengers taken his young sister on the seat beside himself, and loaded in behind his baby brother, for a drive. A rabbit came running past, and the dog, true to his instincts and forgetful of his passengers, gave chase. The situation was rollicking and breezy. No one could look upon that race unmoved and the spirit of fun appealed to all. The men who had driven a similar vehicle as boys enjoyed it heartily. An ardent admirer of these pictures sent by his office boy one day the following note:

THE ART STORE, 239 SUPERIOR STREET, CLEVELAND, OHIO.

OFFICE OF *The Plain Dealer*.

SAY, RYDER: I want you to take those pictures — '' Pluck '' — out of your window, they are making my life a misery. I can't pass your store without looking at them. I've got a crack in my lip, and I break it open afresh every day. I have tried passing on the other side of the street, but on seeing the crowd I am drawn over; the fun in those pictures makes me laugh, and the crack deepens. I don't want to feel obliged to go around a square to avoid breaking my lip every day.

Bill Furst, the barber, hung a pair of those pictures on the back wall of his shop, and one day a man saw them reflected in the mirror in front of him, and got his face so badly cut on account of an explosion of laughter that Bill was forced to turn them face to the wall.

Please take them out and put something serious in their place for a few days.   Yours,   GRIS.

A score of people came in each day to inquire if they were paintings or chromos, and what was the price. Many wanted to know if I was not going to have chromos, and to put their names down for a pair then and there. I became convinced that if I did not have chromos made of the pictures it would be a mistake. So I went to Wellington and got permission from Mr. Willard to publish them, bought the pictures and secured copyright, named them " Pluck " No. 1 and No. 2, and went to New York to find a publisher. I had hopes of publishing through the house of E. & H. T. Anthony & Co., of 591 Broadway, who were publishers of chromos and dealers in photographic goods, and with whom I had been a customer for many years.

With a pair of photograph copies of the pictures I went into the office of Mr. Edward Anthony, the head of the firm. I showed him the photographs, told him my intention, and that as I knew nothing of publishing I hoped his house would publish for me, allowing me a proper interest. Mr. Anthony said: " Well, Ryder, they are not quite the style of pictures I would like to hang in my parlors." I replied that there were other rooms than parlors where pictures were hung, and that I fully believed my pictures would have a large sale. I was somewhat disappointed and went to another publishing house from whom I frequently bought pictures for my trade at home. Here I met a solemn-faced gentle-man, a member of the firm, to whom I showed my pictures and unfolded my plans. He shook his head and broke the way gently to me that my pictures could not succeed. He advised me to aban-don the publication. He invited me into their stock room to show me the styles of pictures which were in demand and upon which money was made. Here, from compartments and shelves, he drew out pictures and illuminated mottoes representing Scriptural sub-jects and texts, as " God bless our home," etc. " That, Mr. Ryder," he said, " is what people want, that is what will sell." I left him and went my way, to call upon an old friend in the art trade, like myself, but who was not a publisher of pictures. Inci-dentally I showed him my " Pluck " photographs, without reference to asking advice or opinion — but got it, just the same, to this effect: " I hate to see an old friend run deliberately into loss, and my advice is that you go back home, keeping your money in your pocket; don't throw it away on trash like that, don't be ' a fool and his money soon parted.' " I confess I was rather disheartened at all this adverse talk, but went to bed that night and turned the whole matter over in my mind. Next morning I went out and found a publishing house that thought differently of " Pluck," so I made the plunge. The greatest success ever known in a chromo publication was accorded " Pluck." The gentleman who would not care to hang those pictures in his parlor paid me for the thousands sold by his house a sum that paid for the entire cost of publication.

PLUCK — NO. I.

PLUCK — NO. 2.

After the successful exploiting of the " Pluck " pictures, as narrated heretofore, the artist, Mr. Willard, brought to my gallery one day a picture representing a scene in a country farm-house — in the living room of the old homestead so familiar to many country-bred people, and which evidently was at once the kitchen, dining-room, and parlor.   The family are represented as on their knees at morning prayers, the suppliant, the father of the family, with a cat upon his back and the two mischievous boys " sicking " a puppyish dog upon the cat, which defies the dog with arched back and bristling tail.   The situation as portrayed was most laughable, and I was convinced at once that it would make a popular and profitable publication as a chromo.   But I also feared that it would not do to publish it because of what might possibly, in some quarters, be regarded as a sacrilegious tinge and which might prove disastrous to its success.   It was after some rather studious hesitation — a vacillation, rather, between a keen desire and a chilling dread — that the thought occurred to me that Bret Harte, who had in many ways shown his ability to skim over the thin ice of public opinion in matters of religious sentiment; in fact, was just then using his bright new pen skirmishing about such ticklish places in a manner quite delightful, and on the line where my present troubles lay.   Hence a poem by him would successfully launch the pictures, as illustrating a poem of the popular author.

The noted personages who visited Cleveland in those days were not allowed to escape the city without having given " a sitting " at Ryder's, and among them was the rising young author of " The Heathen Chinee " — Bret Harte.   Usually it was no difficult task to secure the " hearty coöperation " of the distinguished individuals, and I do not recall that I had unusual difficulty in inducing Mr. Harte to face the camera.   The acquaintance made with him at this time led to a future transaction which, as may be inferred from the history as I record it, took on some complications which in all probability had a tendency to discourage further business ventures with the noted poet of the "wild and woolly West."   I wrote to Mr. Harte, who was then making his home at Elizabeth, N. J., and arranged to meet him at E. P. Dutton's bookstore, on Broadway, New York.   I secured a personal letter of introduction from Capt. Frank H. Mason (now United States consul-general at Berlin), to whom I had divulged my plans, and who assured me of the hearty welcome and ready coöperation on the part of Mr. Harte.   We met at Dutton's, I unfolded my design, and showed him a pho-

A. M. WILLARD, THE ARTIST, CLEVELAND.

tograph of the painting. He was greatly amused, and I then informed him that I desired that the painting should be made the subject of a poem written in his peculiar vein. Incidentally, in working the conference around to the commercial point, it is possible that I may have inferred — perhaps more pointedly than is now necessary to state — that I had gathered from an incidental knowledge of poets in general that the poetic nature of the poet might disdain the thought of compensation; but I may have added that I was not insisting upon the point in this case, or words to that effect. I did not, in this connection, fail to note that Mr. Harte, with a smile, which, while not strikingly avaricious, was quite sufficient to brush aside, gently of course, but effectually, anything that would tend to bind him to my high-caste ideality concerning poets. I could not disguise the fact that commercialism had crept into the matter on my part, and I could but ask Mr. Harte, as a matter of formality at least, what his price would be. When I did so his brow darkened in thoughtfulness, and I could but regard the sign as ominous; and I confess that if I really hoped to find a "*free* lance*" for an ally in the young author and poet, that the thought perished at this juncture. But he was considerate enough to break the ice with me, as it were, quite gently and by degrees; that is, he ahem-ed and coughed considerably and delayed final answer, while I resolutely held on to my chair. He finally announced that five hundred dollars was his regular price for such work, but under the circumstances he would make it easier for me provided he should be allowed to sell the poem to some paper before it appeared in connection with the chromos which I was to make of the painting, and which the poem was to popularize and advertise. This in case he could sell the poem for two hundred dollars and have the privilege of publishing it in his forthcoming volume of poems. This was just what I desired, but the publication of the poem was not to be made until I was ready with my chromos with which to follow the poem closely. His offer was rather more than I had expected, but I accepted it, and he said he would have the poem ready for me at the end of three days, and that I should meet him at the bookstore at the expiration of that time. I remained in New York awaiting the workings of the Muse, and Mr. Harte was promptly on time at the appointed place and had the poem ready for delivery according to contract. He read it to me, bubbling over with laughter as he read; and certainly it was made a successful rehearsal. He had named the poem "Deacon Smith's Experience," but on second

DEACON JONES'S EXPERIENCE.

thought concluded to substitute " Jones " for " Smith "; and that
named the picture. I was pleased with the poem and paid him the
money (two hundred and fifty dollars) and received the original
poem, two verses of which are reproduced herewith, and the entire
poem follows:

DEACON JONES'S EXPERIENCE.

(Arkansas Conference, 1874.)

Ye'r right when you lays it down, parson,
　That the flesh is weak and a snare;
And to keep yer plow in the furrow
　When your cattle begins to rare,
Ain't no sure thing — and, between us,
　The same may be said of prayer!

Why I stood the jokes, on the river,
　Of the boys, when the critters found
That I'd jined the church, and the snicker
　That may be ye mind, went around
The day I sat down with the mourners,
　In the old camp-meeting ground!

I stood all that, and I reckon
  I might, at a pinch, stood more,
For the boys they represents Baal,
  And I stands as the rock of the law;
And it seemed like a moral scrimmage
  In holdin' agin their jaw.

But ther's crosses a Christian suffers
  As hezn't got that pretense —
Things with no moral purpose,
  Things ez hez got no sense;
Things ez, somehow, no profit
  Will cover their first expense.

Ez how! I was just last evenin'
  Addressin' the throne of grace,
And mother knelt in the corner,
  And each of the boys in his place —
When that sneaking pup of Keziah's
  To Jonathan's cat giv chase!

I never let on to mind 'em,
  I never let on to hear,
But drove that prayer down the furrow,
  With the cat hid in under my chair.
And Keziah a-whisperin', " Sic her!"
  And mother a-sayin', "You dare!"

I asked for a light for the heathen,
  To guide on his narrer track —
With that dog and that cat just waltzing,
  And Jonathan's face just black,
When the pup made a rush and the kitten
  Dropped down on the small of my back.

Yet I think, with the Lud's assistance,
  I might have continued then,
If gettin' her holt that kitten
  Hadn't dropped her claws in me — when
It somehow reached the old Adam,
  And I jumped to my feet with Amen.

So ye'r right when you says it, parson,
  That the flesh is weak and a snare,
And to keep your plow in the furrow
  When your cattle begins to rare, .
Ain't no sure thing — and between us,
  I says it's just so with prayer.

BRET HARTE.

Jones

Deacon ~~Smith's~~ Experience.
(Arkansas Conference.)
1874.

'Yer right when you lays it down, Parson
That the flesh is weak and a snare
And to keep your plow in the furrow
, When your cattle begins to race —
 Aint no sure thing. And between us
\ The same may be said of prayer!

X   X   X   X

So your right when you says it, Parson
    That the flesh is weak and a snare.
And to keep your plow in the furrow
I When your cattle begins to race
This in one thing. And between us
    I says its just so with prayer
                — Bob Hurd

FACSIMILE OF THE ORIGINAL MANUSCRIPT.

After I had paid him the money he asked me if I were going up street, and as I so intended we walked out of the bookstore and started up Broadway together. I recall that it was rather slow going, as Mr. Harte seemed to get very deeply interested in every show window that we passed; hence I was constantly escaping his memory, while he was pleasantly whelmed in the ecstacy of indulging the "eccentricity of genius." So, with a cordial "good-day," I left the poet feasting his soulful love of the beautiful on the brilliant exhibits in the show-windows of Broadway.

The poem was, as I regarded it, necessary to smooth the way for the publication of the chromos, which I at once proceeded to have printed; and I intended to have it "blazoned forth" that the picture was an illustration of Bret Harte's latest poem. I desired that the poem should appear in the public prints a short time before my chromos were to be sent out. But Mr. Harte became desirous of selling the poem before my chromos were ready, and I objected quite strenuously. I had furnished the "gad for the lagging Muse"; I had paid the price. I also desired the poem for the purpose of breaking the force of what might be regarded as sacrilege in the picture, hence I insisted upon its publication at the time I had fixed, also the publication of the poem in his forthcoming volume of poems as he had promised. The volume appeared, however, without "Deacon Jones's Experience," and notwithstanding its wide popularity it has never had a place in Mr. Harte's published works, and the reason for it is here disclosed for the first time. In answer to my objection to the publication of the poem before my chromos were ready, Mr. Harte wrote me the following letter, which I still retain in the violet-ink original:

713 BROADWAY, NEW YORK, May 4, 1874.

MY DEAR RYDER:

I received your note yesterday. You remember, I wanted you to purchase the poem out and out, publish it when, where and how you pleased, and for such a price as you could get. Now, the very difficulty which this would have obviated, and which I had foreseen in this joint ownership of the poem, has just occurred.

For immediately on getting your note I had to go to the New York *Times*, which had the poem for two hundred dollars, and get it back — which I could only do by giving them something more valuable to me, for, despite the "Deacon's" irreverence, they had an inclination to freeze to him.

Now, my dear Ryder, I live by my pen, and I cannot afford to wait your convenience to realize the remaining sum due on the poem, nor ought you, I feel, lose your perfect control over its publication. Nor can I, in disposing of it, always indicate the time of its publication without exciting the suspicion you

YANKEE DOODLE — THE SPIRIT OF '76.

(Now in Abbott Hall, Marblehead, Mass.)

want to avert. I thought I was doing the best I could for you by giving it to the *Times*—thus giving you ample time for circulation, as it would have appeared about the 1st of June.

Now my proposition is this: Buy me out. Send me your check for $200, and publish the thing yourself just when and where it will best suit you. You can, if you like, start it West. I dare say Halstead of the *Cincinnati Commercial* would give you a fair price for it. Remember, I should have asked $500 for the thing, out and out, for I feel I shall have all the parsons after me.

Yours truly,   BRET HARTE.

I fancied he was not pleased because of my objection to the publication of the poem at the time, and when he did not publish it with his other poems I was convinced that he desired to suppress its publication altogether, because of the fact that it had been written as an advertisement. Hence I began at once to develop my original plans in the matter, and first had the poem printed in slip form and mailed it to all the prominent magazines, newspapers and other publications, presenting it free to them as an unpublished poem by Bret Harte. It went the rounds of the press like the conventional " wild-fire," and I followed in its brilliant trail with the chromos. The sales were enormous, and the success most flattering indeed.

The fear of the " parsons," as indicated in Mr. Harte's letter, had been mutual with us, but I was pleased to note that a certain good clergyman of our city made occasional visits to my gallery, generally accompanied by a visiting brother from another city. They came to see *that* picture, and — bless their dear hearts! — the laughter they gave to the " deacon " in his dilemma was a diverting offset over against the hard work in their studies. In fact, no one ever enjoyed it more than my good clerical friend. The original painting is now in the Olney Gallery in Cleveland.

The following incident will tend to show the wide-spread popularity of the picture. Dr. Hubbard, of Ashtabula, on a trip abroad, picked up in London a picture so funny that he couldn't help buying it, to show the folk in Ohio what an amount of humor those " Lunnon fellows " possessed. The doctor was proud of his find, and on his return exploited it with much gratification, and continually dwelt upon the fine humor of the English artist. His attention was directed one day to a line of print upon the lower edge of the picture which had up to that time escaped his notice. The legend upon the narrow margin was: " Copyrighted and published by James F. Ryder, Cleveland, O.," and the title of the picture was " Deacon Jones's Experience."

CHAPTER XXIV.

THE IMMORTAL SIX.

THE IMMORTAL SIX.

(Taken April 15th, 1858.)

The following true story of a half dozen boys who in due time " grew up " to robust manhood, is quite unusual and worth the telling:

[From the Cleveland *Leader*.]

There are very few persons in Cleveland today, probably, who remember ever to have heard of a club called " The Immortal Six." But about forty years ago there was such a club in Cleveland, and a clever little club it was, too.

Its membership was small, and, one might add, exclusive, more exclusive in fact than the present Union Club, for, as its name indicates, it had but six members, young men all, and they had some very jolly times together.

Just exactly how the club came to be formed even the members hardly knew. The six young men had come together through their affinity of ideas and the mutuality of their interests and ambitions. They gradually came to meet often and still oftener as time went on, and finally amid considerable laughter and with a great show of formality and red tape they formed their club and named it with all the ceremony due to the impressive and momentous occasion, " The Immortal Six."

The members were William J. Hayes, B. P. Bower, Thomas Denison and his brother Edwin Denison, Charles A. Burwell, and Edwin Powers. They were all of them in their teens at that time, very young men, indeed. History relates and tradition testifies to the fact that they were very good young men, as proper as proper could be. They never stayed out very late at night, their latch-keys always fitted perfectly when they arrived at their homes, and, indeed, one of the members of the Immortal Six said to a reporter the other day:

" Really, our wildest dissipation occurred when some member of our party happened to be a little flush and we all went to Stacy's, which old Clevelanders will remember well, and had pie and cream cakes. These indulgences were frequent."

Not even the plentitude of pastry had the effect of making the Immortal Six other than a set of jolly young fellows, and their reason for banding themselves together went further and higher than the mere titillation of their epicurean tastes. Every one of the Immortal Six was ambitious, and every one of them expected to succeed in the business or profession he proposed to enter. They enjoyed some spirited debates on every conceivable question which makes life a complex problem, and, of course, they solved all these questions easily under the inspiration of cream cakes and the confidence of their youth.

On April 15, 1858, the Immortal Six took an important action. They solemnly resolved to have their pictures taken. This action was not taken hastily, but with portentous deliberation; but having decided to have a portrait made of their club, the members were not slow to execute their intention.

On the same afternoon, dressed in their very best clothes — and these clothes were not unfashionable at that time either — the six walked to the photograph gallery of James F. Ryder, which at that time occupied rooms in the old Merchants' Bank building, on the corner of Superior and Bank streets. The photographer, then a young man himself, was told to do his level best, and he did it, as he has been doing it ever since, and the result was a fine photograph of a fine set of young men.

In 1860, two years after the club had its picture taken, it suffered the loss of a member. Mr. Powers removed to Chicago, where he still resides. He only returned to this city last month to see it enjoying its centennial and to revisit his old friends. Of course he hunted up the remaining five of the Immortal Six. William J. Hayes he found at the head of a prosperous banking institution; B. P. Bower, a manufacturing plumber; Thomas and Edwin Denison, heavy dealers in hides; and Charles A. Burwell, an insurance man of prominence. He himself is identified with the Chicago Board of Trade.

The reunion was a very happy one, and if the members of the Immortal Six did not regale themselves with pie and cream cakes, they enjoyed some good dinners just the same. Incidentally, that old photograph taken nearly forty years ago, happened to be mentioned. That led to the remark that the photographer who took it was still doing business in Cleveland. And so, on July 4th, the same Immortal Six, no longer beardless youths, but fathers and grandfathers and solid business men, most of them with their ambition realized, but their hearts as young as ever, visited Mr. Ryder's studio, in the Garfield building, and had a second photograph taken.

Long live the Immortal Six, and the photographer with the remarkable experience of again taking the same group after so great a lapse of time. He may look up and down the years among the veterans of the camera without finding a parallel to his " Immortal Six " achievement.

He stands today in the very front rank of his profession. His work is known in most countries of the world. He has photographed three generations of Clevelanders, and is as ready today as ever in the past to place his sitter before the camera. Thousands of homes are happier for having portraits from his hands of loved and lost ones. In a way he is a benefactor to the public.

May the prosperity which comes of deserving it continue to be his.

Now, in the autumn of 1902, after a lapse of forty-four and a half years " The Immortal Six " and the photographer are all still living.

THE IMMORTAL SIX.
(Taken July 4th, 1896.)

CHAPTER XXV.

NEGATIVE RETOUCHING.

The most important and first real improvement to the portrait photographer after the advent of collodion was retouching of negatives, which method of finish came to this country from Germany in 1868.

Dr. H. Vogel sent examples of this work to Edward L. Wilson, editor of the Philadelphia *Photographer*, and from him I secured a small collection. The pleasure I found in these little portraits which got their smooth, soft, and delicate finish from the retouched plate was most gratifying.

The coarse skin texture, the pimple and freckle blemishes were converted into fine, soft complexions, most gratifying to the eye, and especially to the eye of the person represented in the picture. This was a phase of art wrought out by the patient German and but recently introduced by him at home, while in America it was unknown.

I expected it would be captured and introduced by some prominent New York photographer, as we look to that city to take the first bite at every pie coming from abroad. I was anxious it should so happen that I could take a later chance at securing it for my own practice.

The metropolis was tardy; I was impatient. I concluded to take the liberty of giving Cleveland a chance, and set about it.

Mr. Cyrenius Hall, an artist skilled in water-colors and India-ink work, who had been some years in my employ as a finisher of photographs, had gone to Germany to study more serious art. To him I wrote, telling him of my want, describing what I had seen, and asking him to secure for me a skilled artist in retouching.

He was successful in finding an excellent man — Herr Karl Leutgib, of the Munich Academy, who was desirous of coming to America. Mr. Hall soon closed a contract with and secured passage for him on the steamer *Schmidt* for New York.

I had a friend to meet him at the steamer's dock, with photograph in hand held aloft, standing by the bridge as he came ashore,

Fritz Luckhardt, Photographer, Vienna, Austria.

A PRINT FROM ONE OF THE FIRST RETOUCHED NEGATIVES RECEIVED IN CLEVELAND.

and see him safely on board the train for Cleveland. For reasons, I did not want him to loiter about New York or visit any photographic establishment in that city.

On his arrival in Cleveland we made him very welcome and comfortable, sounding no trumpets in his honor or in our exultation. Very quietly we.prepared a creditable display of the new work, selecting well-known citizens, among which were beautiful young ladies and children. These we exhibited with pride.

A decided impetus was given our business from the introduction of the new finish, and I soon imported two more artists.

In the spring of 1869 was to be held in Boston the first convention exhibition of the newly organized National Photographers' Association. For that event I made special preparation and took a carefully prepared collection of the " new finish " work, the first exhibited in America by an American photographer.

It was really the sensation of the exhibition, and created a very favorable impression. It caught like measles, and became epidemic. Now came a craze for retouching and retouchers. Great was the demand and meagre the supply.

The soft and delicate effect it gave appealed to all and pleased all. A method which made a person look finer and handsomer was welcome — a much desired and valuable improvement.

I had applications galore for instructions. I had come into a valuable adjunct to photography. I had secured it for myself. Good business policy did not suggest that I immediately open my hand and give to my neighbors and friends what they surely would not have given me.　So for a time I took no pupils.　When I did it was as a courtesy, and never for pay.　In an amiable way I tried to be helpful to friends, but never pledged myself to give complete, full instructions.

It was surprising to learn how many of my applicants could master the art in a week.　Some were so confident of their ability they would only ask for an hour's teaching.　How true —

" Fools rush in where angels fear to tread."

The facts are that the student for negative retouching needs some capital, to wit: A knowledge of the art sufficient to enable him to draw a head from life, and do it well; a knowledge of photography sufficient to judge of the quality of the negative he is about to retouch.　A person possessing the above qualifications may, with patience, judgment and care learn to become expert in this delicate work.　It is, indeed, a rare and delicate work.　The lightest hand and a light touch are required to give a soft effect.　Where *not* to touch the plate is fine judgment; *how* to touch it is the best art.

To so retouch the plate as to make the print from it look as though a pencil had not touched it, but that it was a very perfect *un*retouched plate, is, to my idea, the acme of skill.　In most faces is a surface texture which is precious.　Let us look into the face of an elderly woman.　There are lines made sacred by the drift of years, by sleepless nights over restless, tossing children, by anxieties of family cares, by the happenings of what makes up life; her thoughts, perhaps, following a son in the army of his country, upholding the dear old flag.　In this motherly face these lines have been honestly earned; they are the heritage of an honorable life; they are records of unblemished, kindly character.　Shall they be wiped out with a ruthless pencil in the hand of an ignorant, unskilled, self-styled " first-class artist "?　No!　Get thee back to the farm and behind a hoe; don't desecrate that dear old face.

Let a man who has a mother, who has consideration, who has skill, retouch that plate.　He will soften and not exterminate the lines; he will soften and gently smooth the roughness so carefully as to make it seem a very sweet roughness.

The " mechanic " retoucher I am not in sympathy with.　He will " sheet-lead " a face, covering the whole surface as unsympathetically as he would paint a floor, commencing in one corner of the room and spreading the entire surface.　If he could retouch with a jack-plane he would do it.　Some examples of his work look like a picked chicken before the pin-feathers were scorched off. Again his " real fine " efforts frequently make a face look like a distended bladder, or as though stung by a bumblebee after the swelling had taken effect, showing about as much expression as a hen's egg — I beg pardon of the conscientious, painstaking hen; I was thinking of the porcelain egg, without the pebbled surface grain which proclaims genuineness that characterizes real motherhood of an honest product.

So much have I seen in the past thirty years of the faults and abuses of negative retouching that I have condemned myself to shame for what I was formerly proud of.

Evolution brings us around face to face with what we have thought good and have been sure was bad, that we have a chance to find pleasure or discomfort and take our choice. I am glad to see that the extreme of bad retouch is hidden under something else.

McKecknie & Oswald, Photographers, Toledo, O.

A VISIT TO OLD MAMMY.

CHAPTER XXVI.

LUCK AND WORK.

A man can not live upon the dinners he ate last year. A courageous spirit must be fed and sustained. In his march through life he must keep his place in the procession. It is better that he step upon another man's heels than have his own stepped on. He must keep pace with the crowd of strugglers reaching for the front. He must not be jostled or elbowed from the straight course. He can not halt and hold his place; the man behind would step in front of him.

Verily, it is the persistent, continuous march by which the goal is reached. There may be stretches of level, even gentle undulations, but the sum of the journey is up-hill. It is the story of every active man's life, if ambition to win be the incentive. Fortune and misfortune lie beside his path; he sometimes gets a boost, sometimes a " throw-down." He must be up and off again. He must never know he is " licked." The strenuous element in some natures makes it possible for men to force the fight, to climb the heights and to finally reach the summit.

" There's a river called Luck that runs through our lives,
    But her flood it is sluggish and slow;
And the treasure which by her false current arrives,
    Will never make very much show.

" And the man who sits down by her treacherous shore,
    Vainly hoping his fortune to win,
Will wait till his locks are frosty with hoar,
    For his ship — it will never come in.

" But a far other stream is the River of Work —
    On her swelling and vigorous tide
No place is reserved for the drone and the shirk —
    They must loiter and die by her side.

" And the man who with confidence, boldness, and pluck
    Embarks on her affluent breast,
Will sail smoothly on and catch up with his ' luck,'
    By generous fortune caressed."

There is a place at the top where the successful climber may sit and look back over his journey.   He will doubtless find some defects and regrets, which he can afford to complacently regard as unavoidable incidents, found in the paths of most travelers.

The height upon which he sits is the reward of his struggle—he has " got there."   And the name of his destination is *Success*.

Where one succeeds, many fall by the wayside and fail.   Such is life!

Skill is recognized as the foundation stone to business success. There is another important factor which contributes to success in photography — manners, respectful attention, a desire to make every customer a business friend.   It is sometimes born in a man. When not, it should be carefully cultivated as a sure help.   The man behind the counter carries a power in his work by his manners, if he be courteous and magnetic.   His customer should be made to feel he is receiving the best attention and earnest efforts of the salesman to please.   A suspicion of indifference is fatal to full confidence.

The man behind the camera is another power.   He can attract or repel.   He can give conscientious effort and care, or he can give neglect.   He helps to make or unmake his employer's reputation for excellence in portraits.

He can caper before children and tell the dear, credulous things remarkable stories of little birds and make himself beloved by them.   He can be as tender of old ladies as though they were his mother, and they can say, " What a pleasant gentleman he is," or they can say something else.   Children and old ladies know — young and old men know — all people know a cheerful from a morose or sullen man, wherever met.

The " upstart " young man I am sorry for.   He does not know he is an upstart; he is unconscious of the fact that it " would have been money in his pocket " had he not been born, but since he exists we must make the best of him.

The collodion epoch offered opportunities for study and advancement hitherto unknown.   Many were the formulas and methods.   Some were successful in the hands of certain practitioners, while the same formulas were tabooed by others.   The most successful workers had their followers and imitators.

Mr. Hugh O'Neil, for many years a skilled operator with C. D. Fredericks, in New York City, published his formula for preparation of collodion which attracted attention.   After enumerating the ingredients usually employed, as alcohol, ether, soluble cotton, iodides, bromides, he added, " Mix with brains."

As much value depended upon the careful and exact compounding, the necessity for brains was recognized as a prime element in the construction.

Brains were cudgeled for methods and devices as to how to meet the wants of mechanical helps in printing. Here was a field for ingenuity and invention which was put to work. The query which had been much in my mind as to whether portrait heads the size of life might be accomplished in photography, was solved and answered by Mr. D. A. Woodward, of Baltimore, Maryland, in the invention of the solar camera, an ingenious and simple means of accomplishing a really wonderful feat. Mr. Woodward's invention is very important to photography.

The reaching out of a mirror from a closed window to catch the sun and bring it into a darkened room was the story of that invention. The mirror was attached to a camera of which it was a part. A device for controlling the motion and direction of the mirror, easily operated from the inside of the room, is made to follow the sun continuously and bring the light into a condensing lens and through the negative plate bearing the image to be enlarged; thence, through a carrying lens, the image is projected upon the sensitive paper which receives the portrait or image of the negative.

It is a most interesting process, and to watch the growth of an image the size of life coming from a head of the usual cabinet size or card plate easily lured the enthusiast to a forgetfulness of time and a disregard of the cost of material consumed.

The first solar camera which came to Cleveland was mine. So beautiful were the prints obtained by this device that I kept myself filled with pleasure in making them, even though they were not always ordered. I soon secured the services of Mr. Charles H. Fontayne, of the then noted house of Fontayne & Porter, of Cincinnati, to join me in the production of portraits in oil, in which we did a fine business and which we continued for some years. Mr. Allen Smith, Jr., a famous portrait painter of those days, painted these portraits upon a photographic foundation made with the solar camera, thus giving this class of work the stamp of true art.

So rapidly came perfected methods, modifications and discoveries in these years between the fifties and sixties — all growing out of the employment of collodion — that it was difficult for the practitioner and learner to keep ahead or to keep even with the pace of improvements.

In the magazines published in the interest of photography were given examples of the cream of notable photographic work, which were eagerly noted by the craft at large and served to keep us advised of the progress being made by those we recognized as leaders in the various cities.

A number of men who were especially skilled in daguerreotype and made very brilliant work in that process, did not shine so brightly in the collodion products. A close watch was kept upon the prominent and most progressive men, who were objects of praise and criticism in accordance with the showing they made.

From painting by A. M. Willard.   Property of Hon. John Hay.

JIM BLUDSO.

CHAPTER XXVII.

FRIENDLY SUN-GLINTS.

P. T. Barnum, America's entertainer, who knew that " the people liked to be humbugged," and believed himself equal to the job and held it for many years without dangerous rivalry; who always gave a dollar's worth for a dollar, who stood next to " Santa Claus " in the hearts of children — came into my gallery one day with a friend who wanted a picture of him taken purposely for her who, as a young child, had known and loved Mr. Barnum in her old home at Bridgeport, Connecticut. The printed pictures used for advertising purposes were for the public; she wanted a likeness for her very own — an ambrotype taken by Ryder — and so I had a sitting of the famous Barnum, whose " Greatest Show on Earth " was then in Cleveland for two days. While I was engaged with my work the visiting between them was going smoothly on. The lady said, " Mr. Barnum, I know of many kindly acts of yours, but nothing to equal your exploit of yesterday in the case of the sick boy." A beam of pleasure lit up the showman's genial face as he said: " It made me as happy as it did the boy." The lady then turning to me, told the story. It happened that a newspaper man, a close friend of Mr. Barnum, was troubled because his boy was ill and could not go to the show. " Is he in bed? " asked Mr. Barnum. " No," the father replied, " but he is not allowed to go out." " Well, give him this ticket, Sage. The show opens at two o'clock. Tell him to be at his window." Soon after two, by the clock, the sound of a brass band came sweeping around the corner, escorted by a swarm of boys, and attracted the invalid to the window, where, to his delight, he beheld a " golden chariot " filled with musicians playing bewildering strains. In a carriage immediately following was seated Mr. Barnum, wearing his everyday, happy smile. He lifted his hat and bowed to little John as the chariot halted to finish the tune. Starting again, the elephant, saddled and richly caparisoned, came wobbling along with a group of children in the saddle, clinging fast to keep from being spilled out, and laughing at the rollicking fun. Right behind was a troupe of

HOW LITTLE JOHNNY SAW THE CIRCUS.

camels, one having a double hump and ridden by a fierce-looking
Arab of the desert. The long, swinging gait of the beast churned
the rider up and down, fore and aft, in a manner that threatened to
snap off his head. Then came the ponies — black, bay, and spotted
little beauties. Johnny followed them with his eyes until they
were lost to view, and all seemed to him a delightful dream; quite
as good as going to a circus — even better, for this parade was his
exclusively. He grew to health and manhood without sneaking
away to join a circus. When it happened, in later years, that his
text at morning service should read, "It is easier for a camel to
pass through the eye of a needle than for a rich man to enter the
kingdom of heaven," a twinkle passes over his face — possibly a
memory of boyhood.

His little boy climbed upon his knee one Sabbath day and
asked, "Say, papa, does a camel have to go froo a needle before
Mr. Rockefeller can get into heaven?"

COLONEL STOUGHTON BLISS.

A FAMILIAR CHARACTER.

Colonel Stoughton Bliss lived a life that suited himself. He was the " soul of honor " and of punctuality, methodical in the extreme. It has been said that the city clocks were regulated by his movements. He lived at the Angier House (name changed to Kennard House) from the day of its opening until his death. His daily visitors were many. Bankers, capitalists, railway presidents, men of affairs, business men, and friendly men liked to get a seat beside him and learn his opinion of things, for he was a man of opinions. Everybody knew the colonel, and he knew many. Men and women in distress sought his advice and assistance. Patiently did he hear their stories, and if in his judgment these seemed true they did not leave empty-handed. Others who presumed to impose upon him, found that the colonel could not be " worked." He was peculiar in dress and manners, never changing styles or following fashions. Wm. J. Florence, the actor, a friend and admirer of the colonel, chose him for a model to represent his character of Bardwell Slote in his play of the " Almighty Dollar."

He was always the first man at table and had his special seat; not that hunger prompted, but to stand by his rule. On the occasion of a banquet given in honor of a prominent railway man leaving Cleveland to enter upon more important duties in New York City, the dinner was held in an ordinary adjoining the regular dining room. After sitting three hours at this course-function, the colonel became wearied and impatient. As the banquet was finished, and the doors of the ordinary were thrown open simultaneously with the opening of the doors to the regular dining-room for supper, he walked in and took his regular place — not that he was hungry, but that it was his time and his habit. He was not to be intercepted from the table, or his bed, by any one when the

time came.   He found his match in his washerwoman, whom he
saw but once in fifteen years.   The price was understood by them
both.   She always found it tied up in the corner of a handkerchief.
She knew when to call for the soiled linen and when to deliver the
laundry without disturbing him.

The colonel was town marshal in the days of the " underground
railroad," and a daring act of his was to drive from Cleveland to
Oberlin, the hotbed of abolitionism and the northern terminus of
the " underground," where he captured a runaway negro boy
unaided and drove back to Cleveland with his captive.

During the War of the Rebellion he was appointed assistant
commissary-general, and his duties were to look after supplies for
the hospitals of the northern armies in Kentucky and Tennessee.
For this purpose he ran steamers from Cincinnati to points in the
above states.   The mortality was so serious in hospitals and camps,
that Governor David Tod of Ohio requested Colonel Bliss to report
to Columbus that he might confer with him.   It was alleged that
the bad water was the cause of the unusual amount of sickness
among the soldiers.   The governor referred to this point and asked
the colonel if it was really so bad.   The colonel's reply was that he
could give no information upon that point, as he never drank any
of it.   This reply was considered so good a joke by the governor
that he related it occasionally in his public speeches.   The colonel's
well-known habits of sobriety do not admit of a misconstruction of
his statement.   Uncomplainingly through the last years of his life
he drifted toward the end.   He became drowsy from wakeful hours
and weary nights, and now lies sleeping under a coverlid of green
in Woodland Cemetery, unostentatiously but sincerely mourned.

★   ★   ★   ★   ★

A LETTER FROM PETROLEUM V. NASBY.

CONFEDRIT X ROADS
WICH IS IN THE STAIT OF KENTUCKY,
January 8th, 1866.
(Saint Jackson day.)

MISTER RYDER,
    Cleveland, O.

DEER SUR: That pictur of me cum along as you promist when I was at your
studio on my way to Wingerts Corners to take a last look at the old town afore
settlin down fur the remainder uv my daze — at the x roads here wich seem even
more sootable to me than Saints-rest in Noojersy — wich owin to thet stait going
Republican forced me to move on.   Well now as to thet pictur Eliza Jane dont
like it.   Bascom likewise seems to think it lacking in surtin points of Karacter.
wich men of genius cling to. the world over.   You make the mistaik uv tryin to make
me purty. and every body who ever Knowed me understood that I was not a buty.

II Although I hev been here but a short time — it affords me comfort to notis the Kindly feelin extended me by Bascom; Elder Gavitt; Jo Bigler and others. and on thet pictur uv yourn all the friends condemn it. Bascom ast me what had been done with the terbaccor marks on my shirt boosum and the tetchin joose lingerin at the Korners uv my mouth, you also smoothed out my hare, wich destroid my most strikin pecoolyarity. By placing me as you did you accomplishst one good thing *ie* no one would suspect me uv being bo-leggud.

II Ryder you who hed such a fine reputashun as a artist — for so many years — you hev crushed one uv my fondest dreems uv grateness. — by your crooel pictur. ez I intended placing it along side uv thet most worthy Dimokrat A. Johnson — in my post offis. Knowing thet the record was maid and thet our names would go thunderin down the choridors uv time till Gabrial tooted his last horn.

II I return thet pictur addin the Express charges to teech you a lesson *ie* not to try to improve on nachur, yet I must admit I am grately disappinted in not secoorin a satisfactory pictur — we are crusht

PETROLEUM V. NASBY PM
(wich is postmaster)

★ ★ ★ ★ ★

"PAPA CRAMER"

is the endearing title by which is known Mr. Gustave Cramer, of St. Louis, Missouri, among photographers throughout the country. So picturesque a personality, so modest and unpretentious, so loyal to photography and its followers as Mr. Cramer must have a place in this book, if for no other reason than to silence a thousand mouths with the question, "Where's Papa?"

Here he is from the camera of Strauss. I am proud to present the portrait of this genial man, who is most happy when doing a kindly act for the promotion of photography, or for the pleasure of the "boys."

J. C. Strauss, Photographer, St. Louis, Mo.

"PAPA CRAMER."

The route from his heart to his pocket is a well-traveled road, and "the left hand knoweth not what the right hand doeth" at all times. He is an indulgent and generous father to many. There are no airs about him. He is strictly genuine.

GUERT GANSEVOORT FINN.

ANALOGY BETWEEN SOUND AND COLOR.

In the year 1882 Guert Gansevoort Finn, a most remarkable man, possessing wonderful natural talents, died in Elyria. I knew him well, and stood in awe of the striking genius of the man; a rare power of mind coupled with unflagging and gigantic energy. The lamentable sudden death occasioned a painful shock among his innumerable friends and cast a gloom among musical and art circles, of which he had been a light of more than ordinary lustre. A man of many parts, indeed, and he will long be remembered for the wonderful versatility of talent he displayed both as pianist and painter, seeking, as he did, to wed the two arts to homogeneity, centering his life work on the establishing of the analogy of color and sound. The harmony of tones and the harmony of color he regarded as identical. In a word, his theory was that there was a color scale and a scheme of color harmony that not only corresponded to the musical scale, but was really a part of the same great scale of nature.

Based on almost this same theory there is in Paris a theater where what might be called tunes are played with colors, to the accompaniment of splendid music. In this theater harmonies in color are presented by means of colored lights, and the adepts of the fad seem to derive as much enjoyment from the harmonies of color as from the harmonies of the music that accompanies their presentation. Whether Guert Gansevoort Finn, of Cleveland, was really the originator of the theory or not, he seems to have believed that he was, and his belief led him to the publication of his book, which is now almost forgotten.

SAM BRIGGS AT THE AGE OF 21.

A man realizes, essentially, that he is really a man when comes the day that severs him from boyhood and the interesting period of youth covering the later teens; when he goes to bed a youngster and rises next morning a full-fledged man — a voter, if you please; when the past is looked back upon as something to be apologized for, because — well, because the absolute touch of manhood had not, up to that time, slapped him upon the back or tapped him on the shoulder. It is different with him today than it had been any day before. Of course, he is the same larkish fellow, not disposed to put on airs. But the day must be recognized, he will not see that particular day again; and the boys must know that he has touched par. His nine-dollar hat and his seventeen-dollar trousers, which fit to a spot and pinch him nowhere, must be aired this day, and be shown in a photograph, that some fine day his grandchildren may know that's how he looked at twenty-one. A friendly world is before him and he must step with it.

Many conspicuous honors and places of trust he filled, for many years secretary to everything within reach worth having — all were his. For a quarter of a century he was illustrious grand potentate of the Mystic Shrine at the oasis of Cleveland, Ohio, Al Koran temple, followed and beloved by the great tribe of which he was the head. Offerings of treasure by the bucketful were brought him. Well known as '' a gentleman and scholar,'' as well as '' a jolly good fellow '' by thousands upon thousands, is the subject of this twenty-first birthday portrait. He is now a farmer.

THIRSTING FOR GORE.

"LITTLE PITCHERS HAVE BIG EARS."

commented freely and sensationally upon the subject and readers were filled with wonder and surprise, and the members of our table commented also. The infant listener soon manifested an understanding of our comments, and responded to them by grimaces of a frenzied character and a distortion of his baby face. At mention of the name " Jack the Ripper " his responses in this manner were promptly given. I borrowed

A little boy, aged sixteen months, used to sit beside me at the breakfast table when, ten or a dozen years ago, the morning papers frequently published statements of the atrocities committed by a character described as " Jack the Ripper," in the city of London, England. The crimes were committed with great boldness and daring, yet the assassin could not be discovered. The papers

APPEASED.

him one morning from his mother to make some sittings of him. After making some quite angelic poses showing sweet, cherubic faces, I suggested "Jack the Ripper." He was ready and the sittings were taken. At this time he was nineteen months old. In the first sitting he seems in a frenzy of ferocity, thirsting for gore ; in the second he gloats and seems satiated with his objectionable work. The late actor, Mr. C. W. Couldock, his friend Joseph Jefferson, and Mr. Richard Mansfield were much impressed and expressed surprise at such precocity. The modest, studious schoolboy of today has so grown away from his tragic impersonations as to have no recollection of " Jack the Ripper."

★ ★ ★ ★ ★

UNCLE BREWSTER'S PHOTOGRAPH.

Old Uncle Brewster's photograph — I'll tell the story, though:
'Twas one of those old pictures that they took long, long ago;
His hands were spread out on his knees — how big they seemed to be!
And those old homespun clothes of his were wonderful to see!
They kept it in the album, and I used to sit and laugh
At the funny looking whiskers shown in that old photograph.

The girls grew up, and beaux appeared and looked the album through,
And Uncle Brewster used to come and turn the pages, too:
One day the picture wasn't there — they'd hid the thing away.
Perhaps he knew and missed it — if he did he didn't say,
And time kept moving onward and the years kept slipping past,
And a lot of oil was found on Uncle Brewster's farm at last.

He was old, alone and childless, and they hunted all about,
And at last they found his picture and they fondly fished it out;
They took it to the city, where they had the thing enlarged,
And they fondly, very fondly, paid the price the artist charged:
Then they hung it in the parlor — whiskers, clothes, and hands and all —
Hung it up with Grant and Lincoln, there beside it, on the wall

He kept getting rich and richer, and I've often seen him look
At his picture where they hung it from its gilded little hook,
And I've often seen him smiling as he slowly turned away —
Poor old man! they heaped the sod upon his grave the other day.
They have read his will — his picture's taken down — I have to laugh
When I think of Uncle Brewster and his funny photograph.

                                        S. E. KISER.

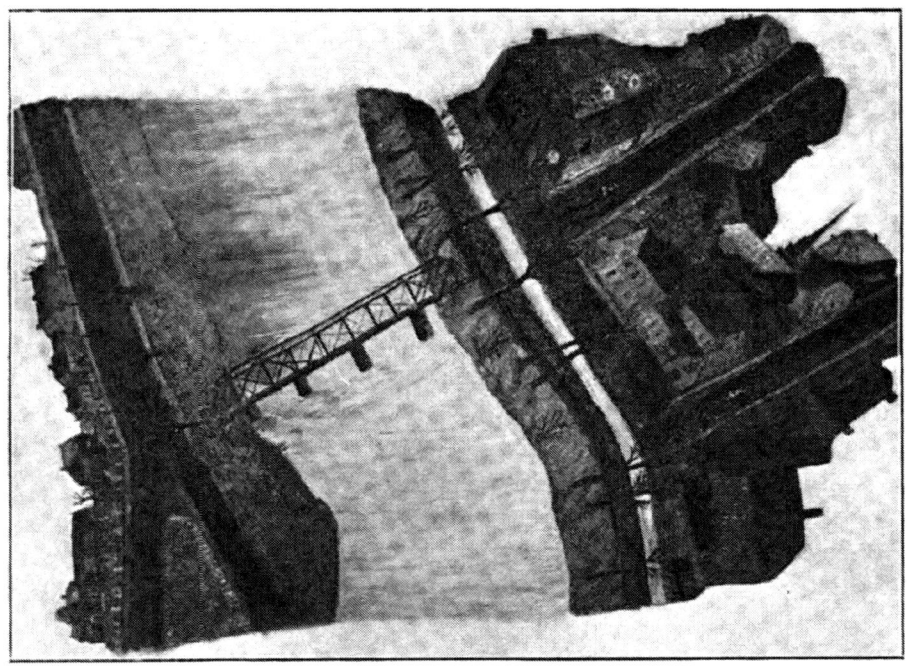

MUSKINGUM BRIDGE.

This is a copy of an entirely original painting; a burst of genius, a hitherto untrodden path leading to a new school of possibilities. It is the work of a young woman of Zanesville, Ohio. Some years ago a project of bridging the Muskingum river at the above named city was under discussion, and divided opinions existed as to the best plan. The young woman, possessed of an idea as to her plan, gave it expression in oil paint. Retiring to the seclusion of her "study," she wrestled with the subject, and proved clearly her claim to originality. And the bridge was built. She took the liberty of "poetic license" with some of the buildings bordering that picturesque stream, an instance of which is noticeable in the happy manner of handling a church spire and some dwellings in the picture. She saw to it that nothing was lost.

The late D. W. Caldwell, president of the Lake Shore & Michigan Southern Railway, became possessor of this unique instance of art and held it as a special gem quite above price.

W. F. Core, Photographer, Cincinnati, O.

GOOD-BYE, "UNCLE RYDER."

To the patient reader who has followed me over the ground of my driftings: I'm right glad you have read this book. I thank you; I am flattered. I have to leave you here. I must run over and see Tom Johnson for a minute — a little matter of taxes.

Wish you good-morning.

"PAPA CRAMER" ILLUSTRATING SOME POINTS IN HIS NEW BOOK TO A NUMBER OF HIS SALESMEN.

CRAMER'S

Isochromatic Plates

have no equal for

LANDSCAPES

Giving finest effect in foliage and clouds. For COMMERCIAL WORK, such as photos of railroad cars, furniture, all kinds of ware, and for copying paintings. :: :: :: Being highly sensitive to yellow, orange and green, requiring no ray filter except for three-color work.

Manufactured by

G. CRAMER DRY PLATE CO.

ST. LOUIS, MO.

Eastman
Kodak
Co.

Rochester, N. Y.

Fifteen years of
satisfaction to
our customers has
made

Eastman's
Permanent
Bromide
Paper

the recognized
standard the
world over

ROYAL
STANDARD
PLATINO
ENAMELED
MATTE-ENAMEL

Fit yourself to turn
out better work by
a course at ::   ::

For illustrated catalog
and further particulars,
address Department X.

Established 1884

McCabe & Company

Manufacturers of the

LEADING STYLES IN FINE
PHOTOGRAPHIC MOUNTS

We deal direct with Photographers

Office and Factory
215 Pearl St., NEW YORK CITY

CPSIA information can be obtained at www.ICGtesting.com
Printed in the USA
LVOW110855080812

293431LV00003B/100/P

9 781279 430194